QUICK TYPING
A Self-Teaching Guide

QUICK TYPING
A Self-Teaching Guide

JEREMY GROSSMAN, PH.D.
QUICKHAND Shorthand Learning Systems
Silver Spring, Maryland

JOHN WILEY & SONS
New York • Chichester • Brisbane • Toronto • Singapore

Publisher: Judy Wilson
Editor: Martha Jewett
Production: Ken Burke
Makeup: Meredythe

Library of Congress Cataloging in Publication Data

Grossman, Jeremy,   1942–
   Quick Typing.

   Includes index.
   1. Typewriting.   I. Title
Z49.G913   652.3 '024   79-26243
ISBN 0-471-05287-6

Acknowledgments

The following organizations have kindly supplied
photographs and permission to reproduce them:

   International Business Machines Corporation
      Figures 1-2, 2-2, 5-2, 5-6, 5-7

   Royal Business Machines, Incorporated
      Figures 1-1, 1-3, 2-1, 2-3, 2-4

Printed in the United States of America

80 81 10 9 8 7 6

To my wife Alice
and to our children
Judith, David, and Joseph

To the Reader

You want to learn to type, or you want to learn to use a computer terminal or other equipment that uses the keyboard. Good for you. This book will teach you how to type—quickly and at your own pace.

This book places a value on your time. In this typing course you will have private typing lessons. Your "classes" will meet at times and locations suitable for you. For that reason you can work at your own pace and study only the material you want to. For example, if you plan to type numbers only in dates, addresses, page numbers, and occasional short lists, you do not have to spend too much time practicing numbers.

MATERIALS NEEDED

You will need to use a typewriter, standard-size (8½" across by 11" up and down) typing paper and a twelve-inch ruler. You may already own a typewriter, or you may want to beg, rent, or borrow one. (Don't steal one.) Any typewriter will do. (If you have a foreign make, there may be variations in some symbol keys.) You may use a manual (non-electric) or electric machine, standard-size or portable. You may also use the keyboard of a computer terminal; if you do, see the table on page ix to see what parts of the book apply to you.

You may use any quality of typing paper for your practice. When you get to reports and letters, you may want to type a few of them on good quality bond paper. You will also need a clock or timer, envelopes (or paper and scissors), correction tape, and paper. The beginning of each chapter will tell you which supplies you will need for that chapter.

If you plan to apply for a job that will require you to take a timed typing test, you will probably want to do all of the timed typings in the book several times each, including the ones in Appendix A. If you plan to use your typing for personal use, you may want to take only one or two timings to find out your typing speed. You will also build good typing speed when you type your own work, so it is not necessary to use only the timings to do so.

How to Use This Book

Because this book is self-instructional and individualized, you can use it to suit your own needs. The following table will help you tailor your use of this book according to your interests. Study the table and identify those sections that are relevant for your interests and inclinations.

If This Describes Your Situation...	...Read These Sections:
I. You have a fair idea of how to operate a typewriter but not how to type.	Skim Chapter 1 and Chapter 2 through page 19. Read Chapter 2 from page 20 and Chapters 3-6.
II. You want to learn to type on a computer keyboard but not on a typewriter.	Chapter 2 from page 20 through the end of the chapter and Chapters 3 and 4.
III. You want to build speed.	Chapters in I or II above plus Chapter 7 and Appendix A.
IV. You are working in a business setting.	Appropriate chapters above plus Chapters 8-10 and Appendixes B and C.
V. You plan to type school or college work.	Appropriate chapters above plus Chapters 8 and 10 and Appendix B.
VI. You know nothing about using a typewriter.	Chapters 1-6 and other chapters and appendixes according to your interests and needs.

At the beginning of each chapter are Objectives which outline what you can expect to learn from the chapter. The Self-Test at the end of each chapter will help you determine whether and how well you have met the Objectives. If you think you already know the material in a chapter, you may want to take the Self-Test first and if you do well on it, skip the chapter. If you are working on a computer keyboard, just skip the test questions that don't apply to you.

Because QUICK TYPING is self-instructional, you may spend as much or as little time as you need on any particular section. The following list gives a *rough approximation* of the length of time you need to cover various parts of the book. Remember, there are *wide individual differences.*

☆ Letters of the Keyboard	10–15 hours
☆ Numbers and Other Symbols	3–5 hours
☆ Reports and Letters	3–5 hours
☆ Tables	3–5 hours

If you concentrate on speed, you will probably reach 40 words a minute (the minimum job requirement) in 20 to 40 hours of practice after you have learned the letters of the keyboard. The time you need to spend to learn numbers and other symbols as well as reports, letters, and tables is *included* in this 20 to 40 hours.

Contents

Introduction

In recent years, changes in typewriters, teaching philosophies, and changing employment standards have made certain former practices in learning to type obsolete.

In the past, students were instructed to keep the copy from which they were typing on the right side of the table. The reason for this was that otherwise the line of vision was obstructed on the left when the typist returned the carriage. If you have a manual (non-electric) machine, you should continue to put your copy on your right-hand side. However, if you have an electric machine, you may place your copy on either side of your table.

Typewriter keyboards for beginning students used to be blank. There are now mounds of studies in the professional literature which show that using marked keyboards is more effective. However, you should do your best not to look at your keyboard until you have completed typing an entire line.

It is no longer necessary to put two pieces of paper in your machine. This was done to protect the cylinders, but today's cylinders will not be hurt without a sheet in back.

ABOUT TYPEWRITERS

The first patent for a typewriter was granted by Queen Anne of Great Britain in 1714. William Austin Burt registered the first American patent 115 years later in 1829. The first machine that typed faster than handwriting was patented in 1868 by Christopher Shoales, and his typewriter was first manufactured and sold by the Remington Gun Factory in 1874. This machine placed the letters of the alphabet where they are on the keyboard today. This is called the *universal keyboard* and it is used not only on typewriters but also on computer terminals.

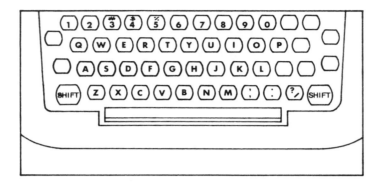

Figure I-1   The Universal Keyboard

The *universal keyboard* is used in all languages that use Roman letters (the letters English uses). The letter arrangement on this keyboard is far from the most efficient one possible. (The keys that are blank in this illustration, vary among different types of keyboards; so do the upper symbols on many keys, especially between typewriters and computer-terminal keyboards.)

The 1874 keyboard had only capital letters (as do today's computers). Typists were required to look at the reverse side of a typed page to proofread as the typing was printed on the back side of the paper. By 1884, refinements had been made so that typists no longer had to be contortionists to proofread their work. At about the same time, the *shift key* was introduced making it no longer necessary to type in all capital letters.

Electric typewriters came to be widely used in the 1950's. On manual or non-electric machines, the pressure placed on each key is controlled by the typist. If the typist places differing amounts of pressure on different keys, light and dark strokes result. On electric machines, the machine controls the pressure so that all typed material comes out the same shade (called density in type). Electric machines will be discussed in more detail in Chapter 1.

By the early 1960's, many offices had *Selectric* typewriters, in which typebars are replaced with *elements* or balls with all of the characters on them. (The term *Selectric* is a brand name, used by IBM. Today, other manufacturers are selling similar machines under their own names.) Throughout this book, we will refer to these machines as "machines with elements." Look at Figure 1-2 to compare traditional typebars with an element.

An element can be changed very quickly, making it possible to use the same typewriter for different type sizes and styles, musical symbols, mathematical and scientific symbols, and foreign languages. It is frequently no longer necessary to have separate machines for specialized work.

By the mid 1970's, "self correcting" typewriters came into fairly widespread use. To correct a mistake with these machines, a typist simply backspaces and types over the same key—"erasing" the mistake—and then types the correct key. Errors in computer keyboarding can also be corrected easily.

Element   Typebars

Figure I-2   Typebars and Elements

By this time "automatic typewriters" also had come into use in many business offices. These typewriters type from tape hundreds or thousands of "original" copies at very high rates of speed, working by themselves while the operator does other work or even goes home at night. With these machines, typists can edit material by adding, deleting, or changing copy on the tape. The machine types all of the unchanged material. If material is added, or deleted, some machines automatically adjust the spacing of the copy on the page.

Portable electric machines made from lightweight metals are widely used now. Most of these machines have all of the features of other electrics and cost no more than good manual machines.

But whatever type of machine you are using, this book will work for you. Where variations may exist, they are pointed out and illustrated.

Now it's time to learn to type!

CHAPTER ONE

Setting Up

This chapter will get you set up to type, introducing the basic machine parts and skills you will need to use to begin to type. For this chapter you will need a typewriter, a 12-inch ruler, and several sheets of standard-size (8½″ × 11″) typing paper.

OBJECTIVES

When you complete this chapter, you will be able to:

- identify and locate several important parts of your typewriter;
- insert and remove the paper from your machine;
- single space, double space, and triple space;
- distinguish between pica and elite type; and
- use the carriage or element carrier return correctly.

THE TYPEWRITER PARTS

The first step in learning to type is to learn the basic parts of the typewriter. Look at Figure 1-1 for the names and functions of various parts of the machine.

(1) The *cylinder* is a hard rubber roller, which serves as backing for the paper.

(2) The *cylinder knobs* turn the *cylinder* and are used to insert or release paper.

(3) The *line-space regulator* sets the machine to type on every line, every second line, or every third line (single space, double space, or triple space). Your *line-space regulator* may not look exactly like this.

(4) The *paper guide* is on the left side of the machine. It guides the left edge of paper as it is inserted in the machine.

Figure 1-1   Some Typewriter Parts

Application

Try to follow the steps below on your own. Then use Figure 1-2 to check your work. If you need help, you may refer to the illustration but try not to.

1. Set your *paper guide* at zero. Place the left side of your paper against the paper guide.

2. Use one of the *cylinder knobs* to move the paper into your machine. Turn the cylinder knob until the paper appears just at the bottom of the cylinder. Then stop.

3. Set the *line-space regulator* at 1 for single spacing.

Now, leave your paper in your machine while you check your work against Figure 1-2.

Evaluation

Study the illustrations of the steps to see how well you did.

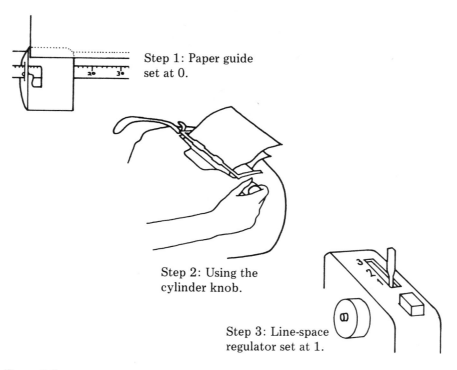

Step 1: Paper guide set at 0.

Step 2: Using the cylinder knob.

Step 3: Line-space regulator set at 1.

Figure 1-2

☆ Did you get everything right? If so, great. ⎫
☆ Did you miss only one part? If so, good. ⎭   You are ready to move ahead

☆ Did you miss more than one part? You should review the material and try the application again.

Now, it's time to look at Figure 1-3 to learn about some additional typewriter parts you will use in this chapter.

(1) The *paper holders* hold the inserted paper against the *cylinder.*

(2) The *paper release lever* allows you to remove the paper smoothly without pulling or tearing. To release paper when you take the paper out of your machine, flick the lever forward. Remember to flick it back each time so you will be able to insert a new sheet of paper properly.

(3) The *shift keys* are used to type capital letters (and other upper case symbols). You will learn how to use the shift keys in Chapter 5.

(4) The *space bar*, when depressed, leaves a space. When you are ready to space, you will *always* use the space bar with your right thumb (even if you are left handed). Some electric machines have a *continuous space bar*, which will continue to space until you release your thumb.

(5) The *cylinder line scale* measures, on the face of the machine, the width of the carriage in number of spaces, or characters, and lets you know exactly where you are typing across the page.

Figure 1-3 More Typewriter Parts

Now, you can do the following application to see how well you can apply what you have learned.

Application

Do your best to follow the steps without help. Then check your work against Figure 1-4. (If you really need help along the way, use Figure 1-4 as a guide.)

Note: Did you remember to keep the paper in your machine (from the previous application)? If not, insert it. Then:

1. Adjust your *paper holders* so that they are evenly spaced across on the page.

2. Use the *space bar* several times with your right thumb.

3. Depress one of the *shift keys* and watch as the typebars move up (or the element turns around 180 degrees, if your typewriter has one).

4. Use the *paper release lever* to remove the paper from your machine. Be sure you move it back.

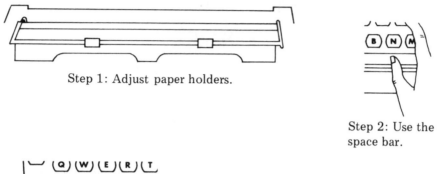

Step 1: Adjust paper holders.

Step 2: Use the space bar.

Step 3: Use the shift key.

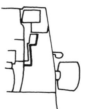

Step 4: Use the Paper release lever.

Figure 1-4

Evaluation

Study the illustrations of the steps to see how well you did.

☆ Did you do everything right? Great. ⎫
☆ Did you miss only one? Good. ⎭   You are ready to move ahead

☆ Did you miss more than one? You should review the material and do this application again.

SPACING

Now you are ready to learn how to space vertically (up and down) and horizontally (across).

Vertical Spacing

The *line-space regulator* controls vertical (up and down) spacing. When the line-space regulator is set at 1, the machine types on every line or *single spaces*. This paragraph, most publications, and most correspondence is single spaced.

When you set the line-space regulator at 2, the machine types on every

second line or *double spaces*. This is easier to read than single spaced

material. These lines are double spaced. Many school papers, from junior

high school through Ph.D. dissertations, and manuscripts are double spaced.

Reports and most rough drafts are also usually double spaced.

When your line-space regulator is set a 3, the machine types on every

third line or *triple spaces*. Triple spacing can be used for leaving plenty of

blank space in an announcement or an advertisement. It can also be used to

allow ample space for corrections or changes in a rough draft, although such

drafts are usually double spaced. This paragraph is triple spaced. Triple

spacing is not used as often as single spacing or double spacing.

Horizontal Spacing

Now, let's look at spacing horizontally (across) on the page. First, make sure your *paper guide* is at zero. Insert a standard-size sheet of paper (8½″ × 11″) in your machine. Make sure the left edge of the paper is up against the paper guide. Use one of the *cylinder knobs* to roll the paper up from under the *cylinder*.

First, you should determine which of the two standard sizes of type you have on your machine. *Pica* type is the larger size. It occupies 10 spaces per inch across the paper, or 85 spaces across a standard-size sheet of paper from the left edge to the right edge (8½″).

Elite type is smaller. It takes up 12 spaces per inch, or 102 spaces from the left edge to the right edge of a standard-size sheet of paper (8½″). Look at the illustration below.

```
                        One Inch
Pica type:        1234567890   (10 spaces)

Elite type:       123456789012  (12 spaces)

Eight and A Half Inches (the width of standard size typing paper)

Pica:

12345678901234567890123456789012345678901234567890123456789012345678901234567890123456789012345
        10          20          30          40          50          60          70          80

Elite:

123456789012345678901234567890123456789012345678901234567890123456789012345678901234567890123456789012
      10        20        30        40        50        60        70        80        90        100
```

Figure 1-5   Pica and Elite Dimensions*

Application

1. Now, make sure your paper guide is set at zero. Place the paper against the paper guide and insert the paper into your machine. If your paper guide is set at zero, the very left edge of the paper should be at zero on your scale. The right edge should be at 85 if your machine has pica type or at 102 if it has elite type. Does your paper end at space 85 or at space 102?   Which size of type do you have?

    If the right-hand edge of the paper is at 85, you have pica type. If it's at 102, you have elite.

2. If you have pica type, type 10 a's. Use any finger for now. Measure the line with a ruler. It should be an inch long. If it takes up less than one inch you have elite type.

    If you have elite type, type 12 a's. Use any finger for now. Measure the line. It should be one inch long. If it is longer than one inch you have pica type.

    Now that you know which size of type you have you can move ahead.

Note: Today there are some machines, called *dual pitch* machines, which type either pica or elite type. Because they are relatively expensive they are not common for personal use. If you do have a dual pitch machine, you can choose to use either pica or elite type.

---

*Please note that when dimensions are too big for the pages in this book, they have been reduced proportionately as in the 8½″ dimensions in Figure 1-5.

CARRIAGE OR ELEMENT CARRIER RETURN

Finally, let's look at the *carriage* or *element carrier return*. If you have a manual carriage return, you should hit the *return* with the insides of your fingers, as shown in Figure 1-6. Return the carriage with enough force so that it comes all the way back but not so hard that your machine moves.

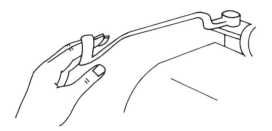

Figure 1-6   Carriage Return on Manual Typewriters

After you return the carriage, depress the *space bar* until you get close to the right edge of the page before you return the carriage again. Now, practice returning the carriage several times until you can return it with the proper amount of force.

If you have an electric typewriter, the *return* key is on the right side of the keyboard and you will use it with the little finger on your right hand. Look at Figure 1-7. (Machines vary widely on exact placement of the return key.

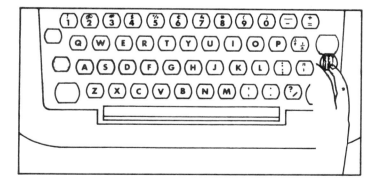

Figure 1-7   Carriage or Element Carrier Return on Electric Typewriters

The rest of this chapter deals with computer keyboards. If you are not interested, move on to the Self-Test.

If you are planning to type only on a computer keyboard, you will not need to worry about inserting paper or about different sizes of type. The terminal you work at will probably either have a continuous roll of paper feeding through the keyboard or a video screen to display what you type. The video terminal is also called a CRT ("CRT" for Cathode Ray Tube).

Keyboards vary among the various computer models, but at this point you should be aware of a few important parts of the keyboard. Figure 1-8 shows the keyboard on a popular personal-sized computer, the ATARI.

Figure 1-8   A Computer Keyboard

Placement of letters, numbers, and common punctuation marks and symbols are the same on standard typewriters and most computer keyboards. Where typewriters have both lower case and capital letters, the keyboard of a computer terminal uses only capital letters and uses its "upper case" for additional special symbols and instructions. Notice these basic parts of the computer keyboard on Figure 1-8.

1. The *shift keys* are used to type upper case symbols and instructions. (The shift key is covered in Chapter 5.)

2. The *space bar* (the space bar is covered in this chapter).

3. The *return key* (the return key is also covered in this chapter).

Again, the numbers and the most commonly used punctuation marks are the same as a standard typewriter, but other special symbols vary widely with the model of computer. If you will be using a computer keyboard, be sure to compare it with the standard typewriter, noting similarities and differences. Also, familiarize yourself with the manual for that computer. The table on page ix of this book indicates what parts of this book will apply to computer keyboards.

Move on to the Self-Test to see how well you're doing so far.

SELF-TEST

This Self-Test will help you determine how well you have met the objectives for this chapter and whether you are ready to go on to the next chapter. An Evaluation Guide for this Self-Test follows.

1. Point to the *cylinder knobs,* the *line-space regulator* and the *paper release lever* on your typewriter.

2. (a) Make sure your *paper guide* is set at zero. Insert a standard-size sheet of paper using one of the *cylinder knobs.* How do you know if the paper is inserted correctly?
   (b) Now, use the *paper release lever* to remove the paper from your machine. Then, insert a new sheet of paper. Did the paper go in smoothly?

3. (a) Set your *line-space regulator* at 1 for *single spacing.* Use one of the *cylinder knobs* to move the paper until it appears just at the bottom of the cylinder. Then, use your *carriage* or *element carrier return* and count the number of lines available for typing. (If you have an electric machine, you may use any finger on the return for now.) How many did you get?
   (b) Now, set the *line-space regulator* at 2 for *double spacing.* Use the *return* and count the number of lines available when you double space.
   (c) Then, set the *line-space regulator* at 3 for *triple spacing.* Use the *return* and count the number of lines available when you triple space.

4. (a) If your machine has 12 spaces per inch, which size of type do you have?
   (b) If it has 85 spaces across on the page, which type size are you using?

5. You had many chances to return your carriage in problem 3 above. If you have an electric machine, you know that the machine is using the right amount of force. If you have a manual machine, did you return the carriage with the proper amount of force? How can you tell?

Evaluation Guide

Compare your answers to the Self-Test to the following. The numbers in parentheses refer to the page numbers where the answers can be found. If you have a wrong answer or are not altogether sure why your answer is correct, review those pages before going on to the next chapter.

1. Check your answers against Figure 1-1 (page 5).

2. (a) Your paper is inserted correctly if the right edge of the page ends at space 85 if you have pica type or at space 102 if you have elite type. (pages 9–10)
    (b) The paper should go in smoothly, if you remembered to flick the paper release lever back. If you forgot to, try to remember to do so the next time. The correct use of the paper release lever is shown in Figure 1-4. (page 8)

3. (a) You should get 66 lines. There are 66 vertical lines (up and down) on a standard-size sheet of paper (11″ up and down times 6 lines per inch).
    (b) You should get 33 lines.
    (c) You should get 22 lines. (page 9)

4. (a) elite
    (b) pica

5. You should have returned the carriage all the way without moving the typewriter.

    ☆ Did you correctly answer all the questions in the Self-Test? If so, tremendous. You are ready to move ahead to the next chapter.

    ☆ Did you correctly answer four of them? If so, you probably want to review the material for the question you missed before you continue with the next chapter.

    ☆ Did you miss more than one question? If so, review the material for the questions you missed. Then move to the next chapter.

    After you have reviewed the appropriate material, turn to Chapter 2 to learn more about typing.

CHAPTER TWO

Starting to Type

In the first part of the chapter you will learn the machine parts needed to set margins and will actually set margins. Then you will cover good typing posture and technique. Finally you will have a chance to type. In this chapter you will need a typewriter and 12 standard-size sheets of typing paper.

OBJECTIVES

When you complete this chapter, you will be able to:

- set the margins on your machine;
- practice good typing posture and technique; and
- type 15 lines of material, using the keys covered here, with no more than 5 errors.

SETTING MARGINS

To set margins, you will use some of the typewriter parts you learned in Chapter 1, as well as a few new ones. Look at Figure 2-1.

The *margin stops*, *margin set*, or *margin reset* keys are located at different places and work differently on various machines. However, a bell rings as you approach the right margin on all machines. If you cannot determine where they are on your machine from the following descriptions look at Figures 2-2, 2-3, or 2-4. One of these illustrations will refer to your machine.

If your *margin stops* are on the *cylinder line scale*, turn to Figure 2-2.

If you have *automatic* or "*magic*" margins, turn to Figure 2-3.

If you have key set margins and have a *margin set* or *margin reset* key, look at Figure 2-4.

Figure 2-1 Setting Margins:
More Machine Parts

1. Remember, the *paper guide* guides the paper into the machine as you insert it. Set the *paper guide scale* at zero before you insert the paper.

2. Use the *cylinder line* to determine where the paper is across the page.

3. The *margin release* allows you to type beyond the right margin and in front of the left one. On some machines the margin release and the back space key are located on the left side of the machine.

4. Use the *space bar* to space across the page (and to space between words).

5. The *back space key* is used to move the *carriage* or *element carrier* backwards. On some electric typewriters the back space key is continuous. It will keep back spacing until you remove your finger from the key. Your back space key may be somewhere else on your machine.

If you want to learn to set margins on other machines, study Figures 2-3 and 2-4. Otherwise, move to the Application on page 18.

To set the left margin, simply push in the *left margin stop.* Move the *cylinder* to the point where you want to set the left margin and release the *margin stop.* It's that simple!

To set the right margin, push in to move *cylinder* to the desired margin. Then release.

Figure 2-2 Setting Margins on the Cylinder Line Scale

If you want to learn how to set margins on other machines, study Figures 2-2 and 2-4. Otherwise, move ahead to the Application beginning on page 18.

—Magic margin —

To set the left margin, pull the *left margin lever* forward and move the cylinder along the cylinder line scale to the place where you want to set the margin. Then release the margin lever.

To set the right margin, do the same with the *right margin lever.*

Figure 2-3   Setting Margins with Automatic (or "Magic") Margins

Key set margin

To set the left margin:
(1) Depress the *return key* to move the *cylinder* along the *cylinder line scale* to the existing left margin.
(2) If you want to change the margin, depress and hold down the *margin set* (or *"reset"*). While you are holding the *set key* down, bring the *cylinder* to the point where you want to set the left margin.
(3) Then release the *set key*, and your left margin is set.

To set the right margin, follow the same procedure on the right side of the machine.

Note: If you can't move the machine far enough left to set your margin, it may be because the right margin is set too close. When this happens, set the right margin first. If you can't move the cylinder far enough, make sure to keep the *set key* depressed all the way to the point where you want to set the margin.

Figure 2-4   Setting Key Set Margins

If you want to learn to set margins on other machines, study Figures 2-2 and 2-3. Otherwise, move ahead to Application 1 which follows.

Application 1

Set your margins at 15 and 80. Use the *cylinder line scale* to locate these points. Then use the *space bar* to move your carriage or element carrier to the right margin. See if the machine locks. If you have a *continuous space bar*, stop holding it down when you reach space 75, and space individually. (Sometimes a continuous space bar will go right through the right margin.)

After you check the right margin, use the *return* to see if your machine returns to space 15.

Evaluation

When you used the *space bar* to move across on the page, did your machine stop at space 80? It should have. When you used the return, did your machine stop at space 15 as it should have?

If your machine stopped at the right places, you are ready to move to Application 2. Otherwise, read the appropriate paragraph below and then work Application 1 again.

For Margin Levers Set on the Cylinder Line Scale

Make sure you press the *margin levers* in before you try to move them.

For Automatic (Or "Magic") Margins

Make sure you set one margin at a time. When you set the left margin, don't let your right hand go anywhere near either margin key. Don't let your left hand get anywhere near either margin key when you set the right margin.

For Key Set Margins

Make sure you hold the *margin set key* (or *reset key*) down all the way to the point where you want to set the margin. If you can't set the left margin, set the right margin first.

Application 2

Use a watch or clock with a second hand to see how long it takes you to do these problems. Check to make sure your margins are correct.

1. Set your margins at 26 and 73.

2. Set your margins at 12 and 77.

3. Set your margins at 21 and 86.

Evaluation

　☆ Did you set your margins in fifteen seconds or less each time?
　　If so, that's great!

　☆ Could you set them in half a minute or less? If so, you're doing fine.

　☆ How about one minute? That's still good, but you will learn to move
　　faster when you have practice.

GOOD TYPING POSTURE AND TECHNIQUE

The last step before you start typing is to learn how to sit at the typewriter
and how to strike the keys properly. Posture is very important. Good posture and technique will make it easy to keep your fingers on the right keys.
Also you will not strain your arm or shoulder muscles, even when you type
for hours at a time.

　　Look at Figure 2-5 and read the key to it.

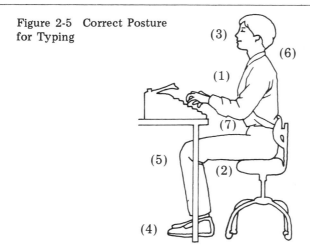

Figure 2-5   Correct Posture
for Typing

(1)　Sit directly in front of your machine. Try to keep the letter H on the
　　keyboard opposite the center of your body.

(2)　Most people are comfortable when their chair is about 10 inches from
　　the frame of the machine.

(3)　Keep your head up and your eyes on the material you are typing.

(4)　If your feet reach the floor, hold them flat on the floor.

(5)　Most people are comfortable when their chair is about 10 inches below
　　the bottom of the desk.

(6)　You may want to move your body slightly forward.

(7)　Relax your arms and shoulders!

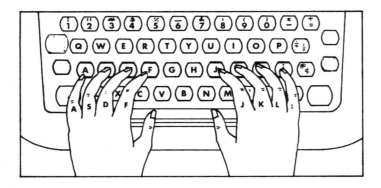

Figure 2-6   Fingers on the Home Keys

USING THE HOME KEYS

1. Place the fingers of your left and right hands on the second row from the bottom of your typewriter, as shown in Figure 2-6. This row of keys is called the *home row*.

   Make sure the fingers of your left hand are on the A, S, D, and F keys.

   Make sure the fingers of your right hand are on the J, K, L, and ; (semicolon, or "semi") keys. These eight keys are called the *home keys*.

2. When you have your fingers on the *home keys*, let your wrists drop slightly, but make sure they do not touch the frame of your machine.

3. Curve your thumbs over the *space bar*, but do not let them touch it. Remember, *always* keep your unused fingers just above the *home keys*. You will soon learn that when you leave the home keys, you will come back to them before you type another key.

   Insert a sheet of paper in your machine and get ready to type.

Home Row Keys, Left Hand: A, S, D, F, (G)

The first keys you will learn to type will be those you type on the home row with the fingers on your left hand. Look at Figure 2-7.

Figure 2-7   Home Row Keys, Left Hand: A, S, D, F, (G)

When you type, be sure to keep all of your unused fingers in place. That is, even though you will type with the left hand only, be sure to keep your right hand fingers in place on the home row. You will be able to type some keys by moving only one finger. For other keys, such as the S (discussed below) you will move more than one finger. It is *very important to leave the home row with as few fingers as possible and to bring all fingers back on the home row before you type a new key.*

Now, place all of your fingers on *both* hands on their *home keys.* Fix firmly in your mind the locations of the A, S, D and F keys and the fingers you will use to type them. Think to yourself: asdf asdf asdf asdf

Pretend to type or "shadow type" the following line. Pretend, also, to space with your right thumb.

asdf asdf asdf asdf asdf

After you have "shadow typed" this material, answer these questions:

☆ Did you move only the A, D or F finger when you "typed" one of those keys?

☆ Did you come back into home position before you "typed" a new key?

☆ Did you *anchor* your F finger in place when you "typed" the S?

☆ Did you come back into home position before you "typed" a new key?

☆ Did you keep your right hand fingers in place even though you were not using them?

☆ Did you "space" with your right thumb?

As soon as you can answer—honestly—all of the questions "yes," you are ready to type the A key for real.

Until you are instructed otherwise, keep your margins set at 21 and 86 if you have elite type or at 12 and 77 if you are using pica type.

The A Key

When you type the A, raise the A finger only and then *strike* the key as if it is hot. Keep your other fingers, including all the fingers on the right hand, in place. Look at Figure 2-8. Then type the line at the top of page 22 smoothly and to a steady beat. Use the right thumb to space.

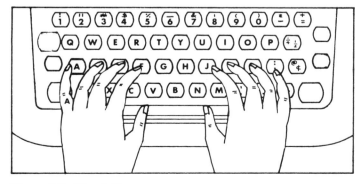

Figure 2-8 The A Key

aaaaa aaaaa

☆ Did your paper look like the line you copied from?

☆ Did you use the right thumb for the space bar?

☆ Did all of your letters come out the same shade?

☆ Did you avoid any unwanted spaces?

If you answer—honestly—"yes" to all of these questions, terrific. Move on to the S key.

If you had one or more "no" answers, you should review. Then retype the line before you move ahead. If you had light and dark shading, you were probably not striking the key with the same amount of force each time. To apply the right amount of force, type to a steady, smooth beat. If you had "skipping," you may have been *pushing* the key instead of *striking it from above as if it were hot.* If necessary, read again the discussion on pages 20 and 21 and study Figure 2-8 carefully before you go on to the S key.

The S Key

Remember, that when you type an S, you must *keep your F finger anchored in place* above the F key. If you do not, your hand is likely to move off the home keys. *Be sure to come back into place with all of your fingers before you type a new key, even if the new key is another S.* Look at Figure 2-9.

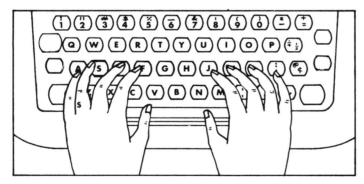

Figure 2-9   The S Key

Now, type the following line.

sssss sssss

☆ Did your paper look like the material you typed from?

☆ Did you come back into home position with all of your fingers before you typed each new S?

☆ Did you keep your *right* hand fingers on the J, K, L and ; keys?

☆ Did you space with your right thumb?

☆ Are all of your letters the same shade?

☆ Did you avoid "skipping"?

☆ Did you *return* the *carriage* with the right amount of force?

If you answered all of these questions "yes," you are ready to move on to the D key.

If you had uneven shades and/or "skipping," practice and try again before you move ahead.

You can already type three words: a, as (and one we shouldn't print). As soon as you have covered the D, F, and G keys, you will be able to type more words!

The D Key

When you type D, try to keep all of your other fingers in place. Be sure all of your fingers, including the D finger, are in place before you strike a new key. Look at Figure 2-10.

Figure 2-10   The D Key

Type the following line.

ddddd ddddd

☆ Did your finger return to the D key each time before you typed a new letter?

☆ Did you keep your right hand fingers in place?

☆ Did you use the right thumb for the space bar?

☆ Did you avoid light and dark shading and "skipping"?

☆ Did your paper look like the line you copied from?

If you answered "yes" to these questions, you are ready to move ahead. If you had any "no" answers, practice the D key and type the line again.

The F Key

You should have no trouble staying in place with your other fingers when you type the F. Look at Figure 2-11.

Figure 2-11   The F Key

Type this line:

fffff fffff

As soon as you can type the line without errors and with the proper technique, move on to the G key.

The G Key

The G key is on the home row, but it is not a home key. When you type a G, you should move the F finger only and keep your other fingers in place. Look at the illustration below:

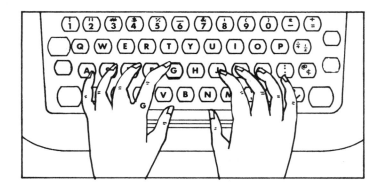

Figure 2-12   The G Key

Type the following line.

ggggg ggggg

As soon as you can use good technique and your line looks like the lines you typed from, move to the following application for practice.

Application

Type the following line twice. Single space.*

```
a as dad fad gas sad gag adds dads as adds sad fad sad dad
```

Evaluation

Your paper should look like this:

```
a as dad fad gas sad gag adds dads as adds sad fad sad dad
a as dad fad gas sad gag adds dads as adds sad fad sad dad
```

Follow the same procedure as you did for the first group of lines. As soon as you can type the material with three mistakes or fewer, move ahead to the next section on Home Keys, Right Hand.

Home Row Keys, Right Hand: (H), J, K, L, ;

The home keys for the right hand fingers are the J, K, L, and ; keys, as you see in Figure 2-13. The ; is the semicolon. The key is sometimes called the "semi" key.

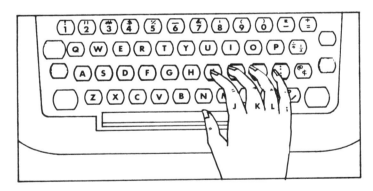

Figure 2-13   Home Row Keys, Right Hand: (H), J, K, L, ;

When you type the J, K, and ; keys, you can probably move one finger only. When you type the L key, your K finger will also move. Try to keep your J and ; fingers *anchored* in place.

Now, place *all* of the fingers on *both* hands on their *home keys*. Fix the locations of the J, K, L, and ; keys and the fingers you will use to type them firmly in mind. Keep your left hand fingers on their home keys. Use the right thumb for spacing. Then "shadow type" the following line.

```
jkl; jkl; jkl; jkl;
```

*Dimensions of many examples have been reduced to fit the pages of this book.

☆ When you "typed," did your left hand fingers stay in place on the A, S, D, and F keys?

☆ Did you "space" with your right thumb?

☆ When you "typed" the J, K, and ; keys did you keep your other left hand fingers in place?

☆ When you "typed" the L, did you return your other fingers to home position before you struck a new key?

If you answer "yes" to all of these questions, very good. You are ready to move on to the J key. If you had some "no" answers, continue to "shadow type" until you can answer "yes" to all of the questions above.

The J Key

When you type the J, move only your J finger. *Strike* the key from above as if it is hot. Look at Figure 2-14.

Figure 2-14   The J Key

Type the following line.

jjjjj jjjjj

As soon as you can type the sample line as it is in the book, you are ready to move ahead. Review the section in this chapter on good typing technique if you have light and dark strokes, "skipping" or other mistakes.

The K Key

There is nothing difficult about the K key. Strike it from above, moving only the K finger. Look at Figure 2-15.

Figure 2-15   The K Key

Type the line below. As soon as you can type it without any mistakes, move on to the L key.

kkkkk kkkkk

The L Key

When you type the L, you probably will also move your K finger. Try to keep the J and ; fingers right in place. This will help you get the K and L fingers back in the right places. Look at Figure 2-16.

Figure 2-16   The L Key

Now type this line:

lllll lllll

Were all of your fingers in home key position *every* time before you typed each L? If you did not return to home position before *each* L, type the line again. If you did return, very good. As soon as you can type the line above without any mistakes, you are ready to learn the ; (or semicolon) key which follows.

The ; Key

The ; is also sometimes called the "semi" key. You should be able to type the ; without moving any other fingers, as you can see in Figure 2-17.

Figure 2-17   The ; Key

Type the line below. As soon as you can type it without any mistakes, you are ready to go onto the H key.

; ; ; ; ;   ; ; ; ; ;

The H Key

The H key is on the home row, but it is *not* a home key. When you type the H, do your best to move only your J finger. Then, snap right back into place before you type another key, even if it is another H. (Be careful to keep your home key fingers on the right keys.) Look at Figure 2-18.

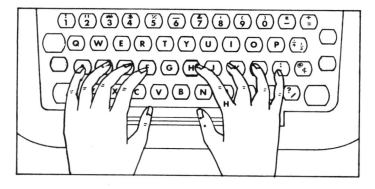

Figure 2-18   The H Key

When you type the H, make sure that your J finger is back in place *every* time before you type a new H.

hhhhh hhhhh

As soon as you return to home position *every* time and type the line without mistakes, you are ready to start typing complete words.

Note: The apostrophe key and the quotation marks key are also on the home row. They will be covered in a later chapter.

Application

When you type the material below, use good typing technique. Don't push the keys. *strike* them. Whenever possible, leave the home row with one finger only. If you have to leave with additional fingers, make sure *all* of your fingers are in the home position before you type a new key. Type evenly and to a steady beat, even if it is a slow steady beat. Type each line twice. Single space between lines that are repeated, and double space before you type a new line for the first time. If you have questions about the format, look at the Evaluation. Do not get discouraged if you make mistakes or have "skipping." Type the material all the way through regardless of the number of mistakes you make. Now type each line twice:

```
a sad dad has a sad lad a sad lad adds a salad as a sad dad

as a gag a sad lass has a sad salad as a sad lad adds a fad
```

Evaluation

Your work should look this this:

```
a sad dad has a sad lad a sad lad adds a salad as a sad dad
a sad dad has a sad lad a sad lad adds a salad as a sad dad

as a gag a sad lass has a sad salad as a sad lad adds a fad
as a gag a sad lass has a sad salad as a sad lad adds a fad
```

Did your paper look like that? If so, great. If you made three mistakes or fewer, you are ready to move to the next Application. If you made more than three mistakes, retype the material until you can type it with no more than three mistakes. Do not get discouraged, regardless of the number of mistakes you make. If you have to, put the material aside and come back to it later. At this point, you know where the keys are and the fingers you use to type them. You also know good typing technique.

Application

For more practice, type each of the following lines twice. Single space lines that are repeated, but double space before you type a new line for the first time. (Use the format of the last Application.)

```
a sad lad has a salad a sad lass has half a sad salad as a

a sad lass sags a dad has gas a hall has gas as a dad adds

half a lass half a salad a sad fad has a gas as a lad sags

a lad has a salad a lass has half a salad a lad has gas as
```

Evaluation

Your paper should look like this:

```
a sad lad has a salad a sad lass has half a sad salad as a
a sad lad has a salad a sad lass has half a sad salad as a

a sad lass sags a dad has gas a hall has gas as a dad adds
a sad lass sags a dad has gas a hall has gas as a dad adds

half a lass half a salad a sad fad has a gas as a lad sags
half a lass half a salad a sad fad has a gas as a lad sags

a lad has a salad a lass has half a salad a lad has gas as
a lad has a salad a lass has half a salad a lad has gas as
```

Does your paper look anything like this? If so, tremendous. If you typed the material above with six mistakes or fewer, you are ready to take the Self-Test which follows. (You are allowed more mistakes in this application than in your earlier work because you had more to type.) If you made more than six mistakes, do *not* become discouraged.

However, determine if there are one or two keys on which you make mistakes. If there are, practice typing those keys. (Use the Table of Contents to locate the material you need to review.) If you have "skipping," practice good typing technique. Remember, *strike* the keys from above, don't push them. If you have a manual machine and have light and dark stroking, try to strike each key with the same amount of force.

When you are ready, type the Application again. Then, move to the Self-Test.

SELF-TEST

This Self-Test will help you determine how well you have met the objectives for this chapter and whether you are ready to go on to the next chapter. An Evaluation guide follows the Self-Test.

1. Set your margins at 12 and 77, if your machine has pica (85) type, or at 21 and 86 if it has elite (102) type. How do you know if your margins are set correctly?

2. Type each of the following lines three times. *Single* space each repeated line, but double space before you type a new line for the first time.

   Do *not* stop even if you think you have made too many mistakes. Type the entire exercise. If you make too many mistakes, you will have a chance to repeat some of the material later. Now, type from the material below:

   ```
   a as sad fad lad lass hall half salad a lad has a salad a dad

   a sad lad has gas a fad has a lass has a dad a sad dad has a

   a hall has gas a fad has a lass has a dad a sad dad has ask

   half hall has had sad sag gas has dad lad gag salad ask gas

   a sad lad has a dad a sad lass has gas a hall has half ask
   ```

Evaluation Guide

Compare your work on the Self-Test to the material below. The numbers in parentheses refer to the page numbers where material can be found for review. If you have more than five mistakes or are not confident with some of the techniques or keys, review those pages before going on to the next chapter.

1. If you set the margins correctly, the left and right margins on your paper should be about equal. (Also, make sure you inserted the paper correctly.) If your margins were not set at the right places, set them again and type each line in Problem 2 one more time. (pages 15-18)

2. Your paper should look about like this:

```
a as sad fad lad lass hall half salad a lad has a salad a dad
a as sad fad lad lass hall half salad a lad has a salad a dad
a as sad fad lad lass hall half salad a lad has a salad a dad

a sad lad has gas a fad has a lass has a dad a sad lad has a
a sad lad has gas a fad has a lass has a dad a sad lad has a
a sad lad has gas a fad has a lass has a dad a sad lad has a

a hall has gas a fad has a lass has a dad a sad dad has ask
a hall has gas a fad has a lass has a dad a sad dad has ask
a hall has gas a fad has a lass has a dad a sad dad has ask

half hall has had sad sag gas has dad lad gag salad ask gas
half hall has had sad sag gas has dad lad gag salad ask gas
half hall has had sad sag gas has dad lad gag salad ask gas

a sad lad has a dad a sad lass has gas a hall has half ask
a sad lad has a dad a sad lass has gas a hall has half ask
a sad lad has a dad a sad lass has gas a hall has half ask
```

(pages 20-30)

If you had five mistakes or fewer, great! You are ready to move to Chapter 3.

If you made more than five mistakes, what kind of mistakes were they? Did you get the format right? If not, look at the Evaluation for problem 2 carefully and type the material again.

Did you hit wrong keys? If so, which keys were they? Did you have stroking mistakes? If so, on which keys? If you had two or more mistakes on any key, review it, and take the Self-Test again.

After you take the Self-Test again, move to the next chapter regardless of the number of mistakes you make. (You will have a chance to improve your technique on additional material throughout the book.)

Now, you are ready to move to the next chapter.

CHAPTER THREE

The Top Row of Letter Keys

In this chapter you will first learn to type the keys on the top row of letter keys with the left hand. (The Q, W, E, R, and T keys.) Then you will learn to type the keys on the top row of letter keys with your right hand (the Y, U, I, O, and P keys). (You will cover the ½ and ¼ keys in a later chapter.) For this chapter, you will need to use a typewriter and have about 12 sheets of standard-size typing paper.

OBJECTIVE

After completion of this chapter, you will be able to:

- type fifteen lines of material, using all of the keys covered in Chapters 2 and 3, with no more than five errors.

Keep your margins at 12 and 77, if your machine has pica (85) type, or 21 and 86 if it has elite (102) type. Double space.

TOP ROW OF LETTER KEYS, LEFT HAND: Q, W, E, R, T

Look at Figure 3-1. It shows that the keys on the top row, left hand are the Q, W, E, R, and T keys. It also shows you the fingers you use to type the keys.

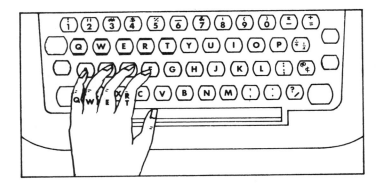

Figure 3-1   Top Row of Letter Keys, Left Hand: Q, W, E, R, T

When you type each of the Q, E, R, and T keys, you should be able to move only your A, D, and F fingers, respectively, When you type the W, you will probably move your other fingers, but be sure to keep your F finger anchored in place so that your other fingers come back to the home position. Let your *fingers*, not your arms or elbows, do the work.

Now, let's do some "shadow typing." Place your fingers above the Q, W, E, R, and T keys, and fix the locations of these keys and the fingers used to type them firmly in your mind. Then return your fingers to their home position and "shadow type" the following:

```
qwert qwert qwert qwert
```

Now, answer—honestly—the following.

☆ Did you keep your right hand fingers in place on the J, K, L, and ; fingers?

☆ Did you "space" with your right thumb?

☆ When you "typed" the Q, E, R, and T keys, did you move the appropriate finger only?

☆ Did you come back into home position before you "typed" a new key?

☆ When you "typed" the W key, did you have your F finger anchored in place?

☆ Did all of your fingers return to their home positions before you "typed" a new key?

If you did everything right, that's tremendous. Move to the Q key.

If you had any "no" answers, continue to "shadow type" until you can answer "yes" to all of the questions above; then move to the Q key.

The Q Key

When you type the Q key, follow these steps (shown in Figure 3-2):

1. Lift your A finger *only*.

2. *Strike* the Q key from above. Let your *finger*, not your arm or elbow, do the work. If you have a non-electric machine, be sure to *apply the same amount of force* to the Q key as you do to other keys. Otherwise, you will have light Q's. (On electric machines, the machine applies the force evenly.)

3. Return to home position with all of your fingers before you type another key.

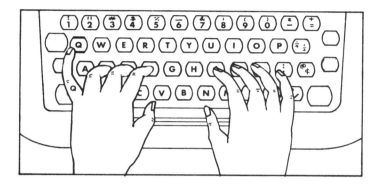

Figure 3-2   The Q Key

Type the following line.

qqqqq qqqqq

☆ Did your paper look anything like the material you typed from? Did your finger return to the A key each time before you typed another Q?

☆ Did you apply the same amount of force each time?

☆ Did you apply the same amount of force as you have for the other keys?

☆ Did you do the work with your *finger* and not your arm or elbow?

☆ Did you space with your right thumb?

☆ Did you keep your J, K, L, and ; fingers in place when you typed the Q?

If you answered all seven of these questions "yes," you are doing well. Move on to the W key.

If you had any "no" answers, make sure you follow the three steps on this page and continue to type until you can answer every question "yes." Then move on to the W key.

The W Key

The W key is the most difficult reach of any of the frequently used letter keys. It is important to *strike* it correctly. When you type the W, follow these steps:

1. Keep your F finger in place. Raise the S finger. (Unless you are double jointed, you will probably also raise your A and D fingers.)

2. *Strike* the W key from above with your S finger.

3. Return to your home keys with all of your fingers before you type a new key. Look at Figure 3-3.

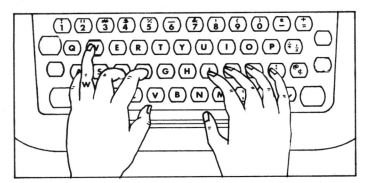

Figure 3-3   The W Key

Now, type this line:

wwwww   wwwww

Did you come back into home position with all of your fingers before you typed a new key, even though the new key was another W? If so, and if your paper looks like the line you typed from, you are ready to move ahead.

If you had stroking errors, remember to *strike* the key from above. Don't push it. Do your best to apply the same amount of force to the W as you do to the other keys. Type the line again and as soon as it comes out right, move ahead.

The E Key

The E key is next to the W key. When you type an E, follow the three familiar steps:

1. Lift the D finger only.

2. *Strike* the E from above.

3. Return to home position before you type a new key even if it is another E key.

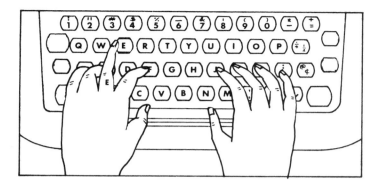

Figure 3-4   The E Key

Type the line below:

eeeee eeeee

☆ Were you back in home position before you typed each new E?

☆ Does your paper look like the line above?

If you answered "yes," to both questions, you are ready to move to the R key.

If you had a "no" answer, use good technique, make sure you follow the three steps above and as soon as you can do everything right, you are ready to work on the R key.

The R Key

Type the R with your F finger. Move the F finger only. Come back into home position before you type a new key. Look at Figure 3-5.

Figure 3-5   The R Key

Type the following line:

rrrrr rrrrr

As soon as you can type the line without mistakes you have learned to type thirteen letters. Just think! You have learned to type half of the letters of the alphabet! Now, to the T key.

The T Key

Move your F finger when you type the T. Be sure your other fingers are back in the home position before you type a new key. Look at Figure 3-6 to see the way to type the T key.

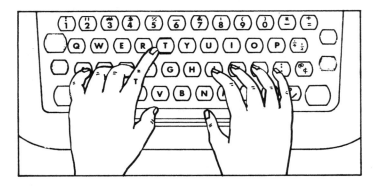

Figure 3-6   The T Key

Now, type this line:

ttttt ttttt

Did you do everything right? If so, great. You are ready to apply what you have learned.

Application

Type each line below twice. Single space repeated material, but double space before you type a new line for the first time. Use the same format shown in the Evaluation. Make sure your fingers are in home key position before you type a new stroke. Now, you are ready to type.

was saw walk well eat ate late real salad adds saw wet wetter

ask wet real reel wells ask rate fee eat fat walk see as rat

we had a salad the rate was a fee half a lad had a fat dad

a sad fat dad a sad lad a fat lass had a salad she was glad

Evaluation

Your paper should look like the material below.

```
was saw walk well eat ate late real salad adds saw wet wetter
was saw walk well eat ate late real salad adds saw wet wetter

ask wet real reel wells ask rate fee eat fat walk see as rat
ask wet real reel wells ask rate fee eat fat walk see as rat

we had a salad the rate was a fee half a lad had a fat dad
we had a salad the rate was a fee half a lad had a fat dad

a sad fat dad a sad lad a fat lass had a salad she was glad
a sad fat dad a sad lad a fat lass had a salad she was glad
```

Check your paper carefully. Did you make six mistakes or fewer? If so that's tremendous. You are ready to learn the other letters on the top letter row, which you will strike with your right hand.

If you made more than six mistakes, don't be too distressed. Determine the type of mistakes you made. Did you make stroking mistakes? Did you type the wrong keys?

If you made more than two mistakes on any key, turn back to the discussion of that key and practice typing it again. (See the Table of Contents for page numbers of appropriate keys.) After you practice the appropriate key or keys, retype the application. Then, move ahead regardless of the number of mistakes you make. You will have plenty of practice with the keys in this section in the remainder of this book.

TOP ROW OF LETTER KEYS, RIGHT HAND: U, I, O, P, Y

The top row of letters on the right hand includes the remaining three vowels: U, I, and O. After you have learned to type these vowel keys you will be able to type thousands of words! The P key and the Y key are also on the top row, right hand.

Look at Figure 3-7 which shows the U, I, O, P, and Y keys and the fingers used to type them.

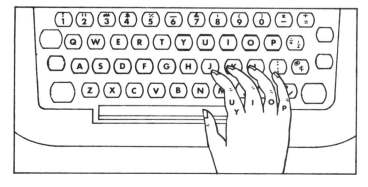

Figure 3-7 Top Row, Right Hand: U, I, O, P, Y

You will probably be able to type all of the U, I, O, P, and Y keys by moving only one finger.

Let your fingers, not your arm, do the work. Be sure you are in home position each time before you type a new key. Now, fix the positions of the U, I, O, P, and Y keys and the fingers you need to type them firmly in your mind. When you have done so, "shadow type":

`yuiop yuiop yuiop yuiop`

☆ Did you move only one finger for each key?

☆ Were your fingers in home position before you "typed" each new key?

☆ Did you space with your right thumb?

☆ Did you keep your left hand fingers on the A, S, D and F fingers?

After you can answer "yes" to all of these questions, move ahead to the U key.

The U Key

Move your J finger only to type the U. Bring your finger back into place before you type a new key. Look at Figure 3-8.

Figure 3-8   The U Key

From this point, through the rest of the letter keys, we will handle differently the lines to be typed for practice. Type the line below twice. *Single space.*

`uuuuu uuuuu us use usual used dust fuse just rust sue true`

Your paper should look this this:

`uuuuu uuuuu us use usual used dust fuse just rust sue true`
`uuuuu uuuuu us use usual used dust fuse just rust sue true`

Were your fingers back into home position before you typed a new key or typed the same key again? If so, and you made three mistakes or fewer, move on to the I key. If you made more than three mistakes, determine whether they were stroking mistakes or if you were simply off the home keys. Practice the line above again. Then move ahead to the I key.

The I Key

Type the I key by moving *only* the K finger. Be sure that you are back in home position before you type a new key. Look at Figure 3-9.

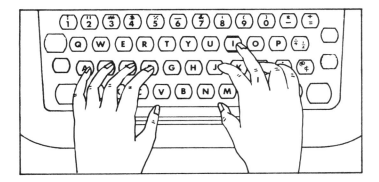

Figure 3-9 The I Key

Type the line below twice:

```
iiiii iiiii aid said raid is it if fist kissed list missed
```

After you have typed that line twice with no more than three mistakes, move to the O key.

The O Key

Type the O with your L finger. Try to keep your other fingers in place above the home row. As soon as you have typed the O, come back into home position with your L finger. Look at Figure 3-10.

Figure 3-10 The O Key

Type the line below twice. After you have done so with three mistakes or fewer, you will be ready to type the P key.

```
ooooo ooooo other doe foe low lower pot taught throw through
```

The P Key

Move your ; finger only to type the P. Of course, be sure you are in home position before you type another P. Figure 3-11 shows you how to strike the P key.

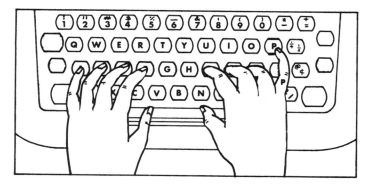

Figure 3-11   The P Key

Type the following practice line two times. After you have done so with three mistakes or fewer, continue with the Y key.

```
ppppp ppppp propeller pet potato put please professor proof
```

The Y Key

You also type the Y with a J finger on your right hand. This is a long reach, but it is not difficult. Type the Y by moving your J finger only. Make sure your J finger is back in place before you type a new key. Look at Figure 3-12.

Figure 3-12   The Y Key

Type the following practice line twice. As soon as you can do so with as few as three mistakes you are ready to move to the Application which follows.

```
yyyyy yyyyy yes year yard yet you your yesterday why day say
```

Application

Type each line below twice. Single space repeated material, but double space before you type a new line for the first time. Now, you are ready to type.

```
you are free to eat half of a salad at half past eight or so

we will stay with our group to eat a salad at our pleasure

did you see the fire at the store yesterday after you left us

did you eat well yesterday at supper did you help with the
```

Evaluation

Your paper should look like this:

```
you are free to eat half of a salad at half past eight or so
you are free to eat half of a salad at half past eight or so

we will stay with our group to eat a salad at our pleasure
we will stay with our group to eat a salad at our pleasure

did you see the fire at the store yesterday after you left us
did you see the fire at the store yesterday after you left us

did you eat well yesterday at supper did you help with the
did you eat well yesterday at supper did you help with the
```

How did you do? Did you type the material with five mistakes or fewer? If you did, that's really great! You are ready to move to the Self-Test.

SELF-TEST

This Self-Test will help you determine how well you have met the objectives for this chapter and whether you are ready to go on to the next chapter. An Evaluation guide follows the Self-Test.

1.   Type each line below three times. Single space repeated material, but double space before you type a new line for the first time. If you need help with the format, refer to the Evaluation. Type all of the material, even if you make mistakes.

```
as a gag a lad of four hurt his dad he was sorry he did so

there is a fat lad who eats salads at his dads house or pad

we will see you at eight at our house we are happy for you

did you see the sad lad who hit his dad with a fat pad as

he hit his fat dad as he was a really sad lad who did all
```

Evaluation

Compare your work on the Self-Test with the material below. If you have more than five mistakes or you are not confident about some of the keys, review the appropriate pages of this chapter before you move ahead. (See the Table of Contents for pages on which various keys are discussed.)
       Your paper should look like this:

```
as a gag a lad of four hurt his dad he was sorry he did so
as a gag a lad of four hurt his dad he was sorry he did so
as a gag a lad of four hurt his dad he was sorry he did so

there is a fat lad who eats salads at his dads house or pad
there is a fat lad who eats salads at his dads house or pad
there is a fat lad who eats salads at his dads house or pad

we will see you at eight at our house we are happy for you
we will see you at eight at our house we are happy for you
we will see you at eight at our house we are happy for you

did you see the sad lad who hit his dad with a fat pad as
did you see the sad lad who hit his dad with a fat pad as
did you see the sad lad who hit his dad with a fat pad as

he hit his fat dad as he was a really sad lad who did all
he hit his fat dad as he was a really sad lad who did all
he hit his fat dad as he was a really sad lad who did all
```

CHAPTER FOUR

Keys on the Bottom Row

In this chapter, you will learn the keys on the bottom row. You will first learn the ones on the right hand. These are the N, M, period, comma, and slash keys. Then you will cover the Z, X, C, V, and B keys, which you will type with your left hand. You will need to use a typewriter and about 12 sheets of standard-size typing paper.

OBJECTIVE

When you complete this chapter, you will be able to:

- type fifteen lines of material, using all of the keys covered through that point. You will make no more than five mistakes.

Have your margins set at 12 and 77, if you have pica (85) type, or at 21 and 86 if the machine you are using has elite (102) type. Use these margins for the entire chapter.

Single space unless instructed otherwise.

BOTTOM ROW, RIGHT HAND: PERIOD, SLASH, COMMA, N, AND M KEYS

As you can see in Figure 4-1, the keys on the bottom row, right hand are the N, M, comma, period, and slash (/) keys. The illustration also shows you the fingers to use to type these keys.

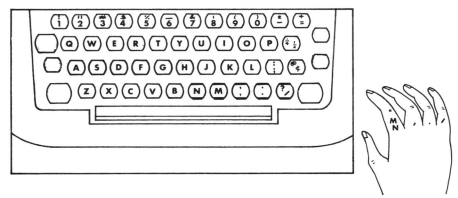

Figure 4-1   Bottom Row, Right Hand: N, M, Comma, Period, and Slash Keys

Fix the locations of the N, M, comma, period, and slash keys and the fingers you use to type them firmly in your mind. Then "shadow type":

nm nm nm nm ,,,, ... ////

☆ Did you "type" the N with your J finger and *return to home position each time before you typed the M?*

☆ Did you use the *space bar* with your right thumb?

☆ Did your fingers come back to home position every time after you "typed" the M?

If you answered all of these questions "yes," that's great. If you had any "no" answers, "type" the first part of the line again (nm nm nm nm). Keep "shadow typing" it until you get it right.

How about the rest of that line? Did you return to home position each time after you "typed" the comma, period, and slash mark? If so, great again. If not, "shadow type" the last part of the line again (,,,, ... ////). Keep "retyping" it until you do it right. Now, let's look at the keys one at a time. Start with the period key.

The Period Key

You will type the . (period) with your L finger. Move the L finger only. Look at Figure 4-2.

Figure 4-2   The Period Key

Now, type five periods. Then, answer these questions:

☆ Did you use your L finger to type the period?

☆ Did you come back into home position *each time* before you typed a new period?

☆ If you moved other fingers, did you come back into home position with all of your fingers each time before you typed a new period? If so, that's great! If not, type five more periods before you continue.

You may have noticed that in this book, there are two spaces after a period at the end of a sentence. You should *always space twice after a period or other punctuation mark at the end of a sentence.*

The Slash Key

You should type the / (slash) with the ; finger. You will probably not use the slash key as often as you use the other letter keys or most of the other punctuation keys. You can use it to type fractions, such as 4/5 or 2/7. You will also use it in phrases such as and/or. You many use it to indicate blood pressure readings such as 120/80, which is read "120 *over* 80."

Look at Figure 4-3.

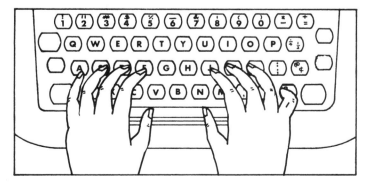

Figure 4-3   The Slash Key

Type five slashes. Make sure all of your fingers are in home position each time before you type a new slash. Once you can do this, move on to the comma key.

The Comma Key

Type the , (comma) key with your K finger. If your other fingers move, bring them back into place before you type a new key. Look at Figure 4-4.

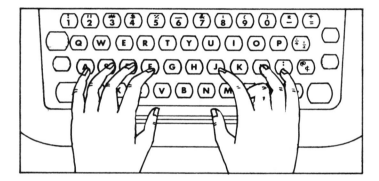

Figure 4-4   The Comma Key

Type five commas and move ahead. You will soon have a chance to type commas in sentences and paragraphs.

The N Key

Type the N with the J finger. Try to move the J finger only. Look at Figure 4-5.

Figure 4-5   The N Key

Type the following line twice:

```
nnnnn nnnnn no not know knee nothing nowhere note neat news
```

As soon as you can type it twice with three mistakes or less, you are ready to learn the M key.

The M Key

You will also type the M by moving your J finger only. Look at Figure 4-6.

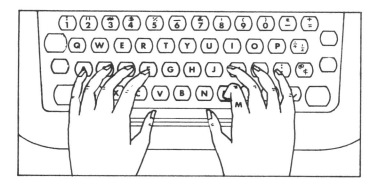

Figure 4-6   The M Key

Type the following line twice:

```
mmmmm mmmmm moon mean mouse meet meat month mow more money milk
```

As soon as you have typed the line twice with no more than three mistakes, you are ready for the Application below.

Application

Type the following lines two times each. Single space repeated material, but double space before you start typing another sentence. If you have questions about the format, look at the material in the Evaluation.*

```
i have learned to type almost all of the letters.

i have only four more letters to go.

i also need to learn how to set material up on a page.

in addition, there are a few more things i need to learn.
```

Evaluation

Your paper should look like this:

```
i have learned to type almost all of the letters.
i have learned to type almost all of the letters.

i have only four more letters to go.
i have only four more letters to go.
```

*For practice, periods are added at line endings. Capitalization is covered in Chapter 5.

```
i also need to learn how to set material up on a page.
i also need to learn how to set material up on a page.

in addition, there are a few more things i need to learn.
in addition, there are a few more things i need to learn.
```

Did you type with three mistakes or fewer? If so, that's great! If you made more than three mistakes, type the lines again before you move ahead.

BOTTOM ROW, LEFT HAND: Z, X, C, V, B

Figure 4-7 shows the keys on the bottom row, left hand. These are the Z, X, C, V, and B keys. It also shows the fingers you should use to type these keys.

Figure 4-7   Bottom Row, Left Hand: Z, X, C, V, and B

The Z and the X keys are the most difficult reaches. Fortunately, they are not frequently used. (That is why they are placed where they are.)

When you type the bottom row, left hand keys, try your best to hold your shoulder, elbow, arm, and wrist stationary and let your *fingers* do the work.

You will type the Z with your A finger, moving it slightly to the right. Keep at least your F finger *anchored* in place so that after you type a Z, your fingers will snap back to where they belong.

You should type the X with your S finger. You will probably have to move the A finger a little to the right. You can probably keep both your D and F fingers in place when you type the X.

You should be able to type the C with at least your A and S fingers anchored in place.

You should have no trouble typing the V with the F finger while you hold your other fingers in place.

You also type the B with your F finger. The B is a fairly long reach, but you will probably be able to keep your other fingers in place when you type it.

Fix the locations of the Z, X, C, V, and B keys and the fingers you will use to type them firmly in your mind. When you "shadow type" try to do most of the work with your *fingers*. Again do your best to keep your shoulder, arm, and elbow in place. Now, "shadow type" the following line:

zxcvb zxcvb zxcvb zxcvb

☆ Did you return to home position before you shadow typed each new key?

☆ Did you let your fingers do most of the work?

☆ Did you shadow type each key with the same amount of force you used to type other keys?

When you can answer these questions "yes," you are ready to practice typing the Z key.

The Z Key

Remember to type the Z with the A finger. Anchor at least your F finger in place. Return to home position before you type each new key. Look at Figure 4-8.

Figure 4-8   The Z Key

Since the Z and the X are used less frequently than other letters, the practice lines for these two letters will be combined.

The X Key

Type the X with the S finger. Keep at least your F finger in place. Look at Figure 4-9.

Figure 4-9   The X Key

Now, type this line twice:

```
zzzzz xxxxx zzzzz xxxxx xylophone zealous zinc zero xenia zone
```

As soon as you can type the line with three mistakes or fewer, move ahead to the C key.

The C Key

Type the C with your D finger. Keep your A and S fingers anchored in place, as you see in Figure 4-10.

Figure 4-10   The C Key

Type the following line two times:

```
ccccc ccccc come company contrast cease church choose comma
```

Move ahead when you type the line twice with three mistakes or less.

The V Key

You should have no trouble typing the V with your F finger. Your other fingers will remain in place as you see in Figure 4-11.

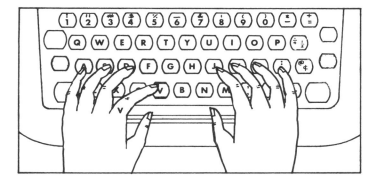

Figure 4-11   The V Key

Type this line twice:

```
vvvvv vvvvv very ever vote vine view every various very viola
```

As soon as you have typed the line twice with as few as three mistakes, move to the B key—the last of the letter keys.

The B Key

Type the B with your F finger. You can probably keep your other fingers in place. If you can't, keep at least your A and S fingers anchored in place. Look at Figure 4-12.

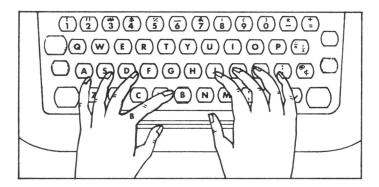

Figure 4-12   The B Key

Type this line twice:

```
bbbbb bbbbb big boy blow brown blown build built bay bath bill
```

After you type the line twice with three mistakes or fewer, you are ready for the next Application.

Application

Type each line of the following material twice. Single space repeated lines, but leave an extra line space before you type each sentence for the first time. If you have questions about the format, look at the Evaluation on pages 49-50.

```
i know how to type all of the letters of the alphabet.

that is good enough if i plan to work on computer keyboards.

however, i should practice on chapter seven, the timings.

for typing, i have a few more things i need to learn.
```

Evaluation

How did you do? If you typed with no more than three mistakes, you are ready to take the Self-Test. If you made more than three mistakes, repeat the Application and then take the Self-Test.

SELF-TEST

This Self-Test will help you determine how well you have met the objective for this chapter and whether you are ready to go on to the next chapter. An Evaluation Guide follows.

Type each line three times. Single space repeated lines, but leave an extra line before you type a new line for the first time. If you really have questions about the format, look at the evaluation. Now, you are ready to type.

```
for many years, the populations of many cities declined.

in recent years, the trend has been reversed in many cities.

some cities have new office buildings and stores downtown.

some also have new apartments, shops and restaurants.

a suprising number of cities have new convention centers.
```

Evaluation

Your paper should look something like this:

```
for many years, the populations of many cities declined.
for many years, the populations of many cities declined.
for many years, the populations of many cities declined.

in recent years, the trend has been reversed in many cities.
in recent years, the trend has been reversed in many cities.
in recent years, the trend has been reversed in many cities.

some cities have new office buildings and stores downtown.
some cities have new office buildings and stores downtown.
some cities have new office buildings and stores downtown.

some also have new apartments, shops and restaurants.
some also have new apartments, shops and restaurants.
some also have new apartments, shops and restaurants.

a surprising number of cities have new convention centers.
a surprising number of cities have new convention centers.
a surprising number of cities have new convention centers.
```

Check your work carefully. If you made five mistakes or fewer, you are ready to begin the next chapter. If you made more than five mistakes, type the application material again before you move ahead.

CHAPTER FIVE

Typing Capital Letters, Indenting, Proofreading, and Correcting

In this chapter you will learn to type capitals and indent. After that, you will have a chance to proofread to locate mistakes and to make neat corrections.

For this chapter, you will need a typewriter and about 12 sheets of standard-size typing paper. You will also need *correction tape* or *correction paper*. You may, but are not required to, use *white out fluid* and/or a *typewriter eraser*. If you're not sure exactly what these are, look at the section just below the objectives.

OBJECTIVES

After completing this chapter, you will be able to:

- type five names which have several capital letters (with no more than two "flying capitals");
- neatly correct all stroking mistakes;
- indent to start paragraphs; and
- proofread ten sentences to identify most types of mistakes.

MATERIALS FOR MAKING CORRECTIONS

The following discussion will identify *correction paper, correction tape, correction fluid*, and *typewriter erasers* so you know what you are looking for. The advantages and limitations of these materials, and the proper usage of them, will be discussed later in the chapter.

Correction Paper

Correction paper is paper with a white, chalk-like film on one side. When using correction paper, you should move your carriage or element carrier back to where the error occurred, and insert the correction paper (film side down) over the letter(s) you wish to correct. Next retype the same mistake key(s), and they should disappear. Then backspace again, type the correct key or keys, and continue to type.

Correction Tape

Correction tape is a white adhesive tape that you place over a line or lines you wish to retype. The material is then retyped on the tape itself.

Correction Fluid

Correction fluid is a fast-drying liquid used to cover mistakes. After the fluid dries, continue typing right over the fluid. (Make sure you wait until the fluid dries.)

Typewriter Erasers

There are several types of *typewriter erasers.* If you want to use an eraser, you should probably check with an office or school supply store to choose one that best suits your purpose.

CAPITALIZATION

If you have a typewriter where the carriage moves (a machine that doesn't have an element), look at Figure 5-1.

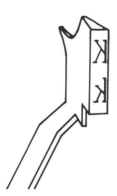

Figure 5-1   Capitals on Machines with Typebars

Notice that capital letters appear on the top part of each *typebar* and small letters on the lower part.

If you have a machine with an element look at Figure 5-2.

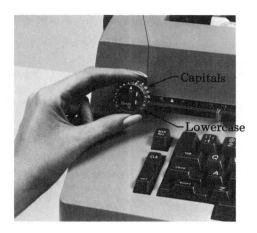

Figure 5-2   Capitals on Machines with Elements

Notice that *capital* letters appear on one side of the *element* and the corresponding small letters appear exactly 180 degrees on the other side of the element.

If you are using a computer keyboard, you do not have capitals. Instead, the shift key is used for special computer symbols and instructions, which vary widely among computer models. Check the operators manual, and modify the following instructions about how to use the *shift key* as you practice using the shift key for your particular model.

Remember where your shift keys are? If not, refer to Figure 1-3 on page 7.

You will soon learn how to correctly depress the *shift keys*. Now, however, use any finger to depress one of the shift keys. Notice what happens to your machine.

If you have a machine with typebars, watch the entire row of typebars *shift* up.

If you have a machine with an element, watch the element *shift* around 180 degrees.

Using the Shift Key

Always *shift* the machine to type capitals with the *opposite* hand from the one you need to type the capital letter. For example, when you want to type a capital A, use the shift key on the right side of the machine. To type a capital J, use the shift key on the left side of the typewriter.

Look at Figure 5-3. When you depress the shift key on the left hand, keep your F finger in place above the F key. Depress the shift key with the A finger. When you are ready to release the shift key, your other fingers will easily find their home positions.

Figure 5-3   Using the Left Hand Shift Key

Now, look at Figure 5-4. When you depress the shift key on the right side of your machine, anchor your J finger in place above the J key. Use the ; finger to depress the shift key. If you keep your J finger firmly in place, your other fingers will return to home position when you release the shift key.

Figure 5-4   Using the Right Hand Shift Key

Four Steps in Typing Capital Letters

There are *four separate steps* in typing a capital letter. It is important to *follow them in sequence* and to fully complete each step before you start on the next one. It might help you to "shadow type" several letters with each hand as you read these steps.

1. *Depress* the shift key on the *opposite* hand. Make sure your F or J finger is firmly in place. Then *hold* the shift key all the way down.

2. *Type* the capital letter you want, *only after the shift key is all the way down.*

3. *Release* the shift key, *only after you have typed the capital letter.*

4. *Come back into home position* with the fingers on both your shift key and capital letter hands before you type a new stroke.

Application

When you type the line below, be sure you follow the four steps. Be sure that all of your fingers are in home position before you type a new key. Type the following line:

A   S   D   F

Evaluation

☆ Did you use the shift key on your *right* hand?

☆ Did you keep your J finger firmly in place?

☆ Was the shift key *all the way down* when you typed each letter?

☆ Were *all* of your fingers back in home position before you typed a new letter?

☆ Did you avoid "flying capitals"? (See Figure 5-5).

If you did everything right that's great. If not, type the line again.

This Is To lllustrate Flying Capitals

Figure 5-5 "Flying Capitals"

Application

Now, type this line:

J   K   L   J   K   L

Evaluation

☆ Did you use the shift key on the *left hand?*

☆ Did you keep your F finger firmly in place?

☆ Was the shift key *all the way down* when you typed each letter?

☆ Were *all* of your fingers back in home position before you typed a new letter?

☆ Did you avoid "flying capitals"?

If you did everything right, that's tremendous! If you made mistakes, try again.

Soon, you will use capital letters to type sentences. But, now let's learn indenting.

INDENTING

Today, several acceptable styles are used for typing reports and letters. One, the Block Style, which you will learn about later, does not require indenting. Other styles, however, do use indenting.

When you indent for a new paragraph, you will usually indent five spaces. However, sometimes in business, paragraphs are indented seven or even ten spaces.

The mechanics of indenting are simple. First, you need to know the locations of three more machine parts, the *tabulator*, the *tabulator set*, and the *tabulator clear* keys. The last two parts are generally called the *tab set* and *tab clear* keys. The key locations on many manuals and many electrics are shown in Figure 5-6. The location of keys on most machines with an element is shown in Figure 5-7. These keys may be different places on your machine. Check yours for their location.

Figure 5-6   Indenting on Many Manual Machines and Many Electrics

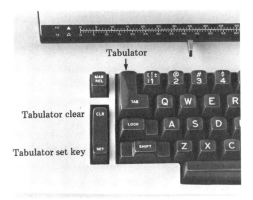

Figure 5-7   Indenting on Most Machines with an Element

When you want to set the machine to indent, follow these steps in sequence:

1. Depress the *tabulator* or tab key.

2. If the machine stops before the right margin, depress the *tab clear* or *clear* key each time it stops. Then *return* the *carriage* or *element carrier* to the left margin.

3. Depress the *tabulator* or *tab* key again. Your *carriage* or *element carrier* should move to the right margin. If it does not, repeat step 2. Then *return* the *carriage* or *element carrier* to the left margin.

4. Use the *space bar* to bring the *carriage* or *element* to the place you want the machine to stop for indenting. (Assume your left margin is at space 21 and that you want to indent five spaces when you begin a new paragraph. Use the space bar to go to space 26.) At that point, depress the *tab set* or *set* key. Return the carriage or element to the left margin.

5. Depress the *tabulator* or *tab* key again. Your machine should stop at space 26. When you depress the *tabulator* or *tab* key again, your machine should make a nonstop trip to the right margin. If it does, great. If not, start from step 1 and repeat the process again. If it still doesn't work, ask for help.
   Return your *carriage* or *element* to the left margin.

6. Each time you want to indent depress the *tabulator* or *tab* key.

Application

Make sure your margins are set at 12 and 77; if you have pica type, or at 21 and 86 if you have elite. Indent each paragraph five spaces. Remember to space twice after periods at the ends of sentences. Now type the following material.

```
        Today, in some styles, there is no indenting at all.
In other styles, new paragraphs are indented for seven or
ten spaces.  In this book, some of the material will not be
indented.  Other material will be indented five spaces.  There
will be no indenting of more than five spaces except in
typing data in the form of columns.
        Later in this book, I will learn to use the tabulator,
tab set, and tab clear keys in typing columns and tables.
This should be fun.  I can hardly wait.
        I wish I could practice more indenting now.  However,
I will have to wait until I learn to type reports and tables.
```

Evaluation

☆ How did you do?

☆ Did you indent correctly? You did? Great!

☆ How did you do with your capital letters?

☆ Did you use your L finger to type the period?

☆ Did you space twice after periods at the ends of sentences?

If you did all of these, that's terrific! If not, type the material again.
Now, if you wish, set the machine to indent for seven and ten spaces.
Then use the tabulator to see whether it stops at the right place.
Then move to the section on proofreading.

PROOFREADING

Before you make corrections, you have to identify your mistakes. To do
this, you need to proofread carefully what you have typed. This section will
introduce briefly some common errors in typing. You should proofread
before you have taken the paper out of your machine. You will find it quite
difficult to line your work up for corrections if you don't. Now read the following material and circle errors where corrections need to be made. There
may be some lines where no corrections are needed. Do your work in this
book.

Application

1. Is a correction require ni this sentence?

2. How about this sentence?

3. Carefully read whay the cheif said.

4. Is their a correction that should be made in this line.

5. How about this one?

Evaluation

You should have marked the lines like this:

1. Is a correction (require ni) this sentence?

2. How about this sentence?

3. Carefully read (whay) the (cheif) said.

4. Is (their) a correction that should be made in this line(.)

5. How about this one?

There are six types of mistakes in this Application. In line 1, letters were transposed. "ni" should be "in." There was also a mistake in grammar. "Require" should be "required." There were no mistakes in line 2. In line 3, an adjacent key was used and there was a misspelling: "whay" should have been "what," and "cheif" should have been "chief." In line 4, a word that can be spelled more than one way was misspelled. "their" should have been "there." There were no mistakes in line 5.

Did you find all the mistakes? If so, great. But, try the sentences below anyway. If you missed finding some mistakes, look carefully at the next group of sentences and be careful not to miss the same kind of mistake again. Circle where a correction has to be made. There may be sentences where there are no corrections needed. You can do your work in this book.

Application 2

1. I do not know weather he will be able to attend.

2. Use your own judgement.

3. I hope the plane will arrive on time.

4. Will he be hte first to come.

5. Is therw a mistake in this sentence.

Evaluation

Your paper should look like this:

1. I do not know (weather) he will be able to attend.

2. Use your own (judgement).

3. I hope the plane will arrive on time.

4. Will he be (hte) first to come.

5. Is (therw) a mistake in this sentence.

Sentence 1 has a spelling mistake. Context tells us that the correct spelling for the fourth word is "whether." Another spelling mistake appears in sentence 2. The last word should be spelled "judgment." There is no "e." There is no mistake in sentence 3. Sentences 4 and 5 should end with question marks. In addition, sentence 4 contains transposed letters for the word "the" and sentence 5 has a key adjacent to the correct one in the second word, which should be "there."

Did you find all six mistakes? If so, very good. If not, be more careful to locate the kinds of mistakes you missed.

Now, you are ready to learn different techniques for making corrections.

MAKING CORRECTIONS

Today, there is some computer equipment which can correct "typed" material itself. We will discuss this equipment first, Then we will learn about different types of corrections on everyday machines.

On Typewriter Keyboards on Most Computer Terminals

When you type on a typewriter keyboard into a computer and want to make a correction, you usually simply back space to the place where you want to make the correction and then type the correct key. There is no need to "erase." It's that simple.

On Self-Correcting Typewriters

(Skip ahead to the next section if you don't have a self-correcting machine.)
On self-correcting typewriters you can correct mistakes quickly and neatly. You don't have to worry about pieces of your eraser or fluid getting all over the typewriter. Because self-correcting machines are expensive, they are more common in business than for personal use. With a self-correcting typewriter, you can correct originals but not carbons. (Of course, you can use a copying machine instead of carbon paper and just correct the master copy before you make machine copies.) It's usually not practical to correct a mistake of more than a few strokes on a self-correcting machine. Let's look at the outline and the steps below to see how to make corrections on self-correcting machines.

Step 1:   Find the *correction key* on your machine. On most self-correcting equipment it is on the right side of the machine. Depress this key until your carriage or element carrier is at the place where you want to make the correction..

Step 2:   Type the *wrong* key again. As you do this, the machine will "lift off" the mistake.

Step 3:   Type the correct key. The typed material should come out correctly.

On Other Typewriters

Now, let's look at four methods of making corrections on ordinary machines. There are advantages and disadvantages of each method. Some correction methods are appropriate for some corrections and not for others. We'll discuss the kinds of corrections each method is best suited for. In addition, you will learn the steps to take in using each of the four methods.

Correction Paper

Do you remember what *correction paper* is? Don't confuse it with correction tape. Correction paper is suitable for corrections of up to five strokes. It is generally not used for longer corrections. It corrects originals but not carbons. Of course, if you plan to use a copying machine instead of carbons, all you need to correct is the original.

Correction paper is much neater than an eraser or correction fluid. You don't have to worry about getting your machine (and yourself) messy. You do not have to wait for anything to dry. A disadvantage is that it sometimes does not "lift off" the error completely. In addition, you sometimes have to type the correct key three or four times to get it to the same shade as the rest of your typed material.

When you use correction paper, follow these steps.in sequence.

1. Backspace to the point where you want to make the correction.

2. Insert a piece of correction paper over the letter(s) to be corrected.

3. Type the *wrong* key or keys again. This will "lift off" the error.

4. Backspace again and type the correct key or keys.

5. Move the carriage or element carrier to the point where you want to continue typing. Easy, isn't it?

Now, look at some other methods of making corrections. After you have reviewed several methods, you will have a chance to apply what you have learned.

Correction Tape

Do you remember what *correction tape* is? Correction tape is appropriate for long changes. It comes in many sizes and is occasionally used on almost an entire page. The use of the tape is not too detectable on machine made copies, however, it is obvious on original copies and on carbons. Simply place the self-sticking tape over the material you want to change and type the corrected material right on it.

Correction Fluid

Correction fluid is used frequently. It is appropriate for both short and long corrections. It, too, appears obviously on carbon copies. If it is applied *neatly* it cannot be detected on original copies. One other advantage is that some manufacturers have come out with a line of correction fluid in colors to match the many shades of paper. You must, however, wait for the fluid to dry before you type over it. If you are not careful, you may end up with the fluid on your typewriter. When you use correction fluid simply follow these steps.

1. Apply the fluid to the place you want to cover.

2. Wait for it to dry completely.

3. Type over the corrected portion and continue merrily along your way.

Erasers

Erasing is still sometimes used, but it is not required in this course. You will understand the disadvantages of erasing as you read through the following steps.

1. Use a *hard eraser* on the original copy.

2. Use a *soft eraser* on *carbon* copies.

3. Make sure the erasers and your hands are clean.

4. Turn the paper until the material to be erased shows at the top of the cylinder.

5. Move the carriage to one side so that the eraser "grit" does not fall into your machine. (If your machine has typebars, you have to be particularly careful. Grit can fall between the typebars and interfere with their movement.)

6. *Start* erasing with the *last carbon* copy. (Be sure to use a *soft* eraser on the carbon.) Always insert a strip of paper between the erasure and the shiny side of the carbon paper and leave it in place until you've finished all the erasing.

7. Then work backwards from the carbon copy to the original.

8. Use the *hard* eraser on the original. Blow the grit away from your machine.

9. Remove the strips of paper.

10. Return the carriage to the point where the erasure was made.

11. If necessary, backspace and type again until the letter is as dark as the rest of the material you have typed on the page.

General Comments on Corrections

You will often use more than one method of correction on the same page. For example, you may use correction paper for short corrections and correction tape for longer ones. In addition, you may use one procedure when it is more important that the original be clean than that the copies be clean. Correction paper is recommended for short corrections and correction tape for longer ones. However, you may want to experiment to see which methods work best for you.

Application

Circle any material that has to be corrected in the following sentences. Do your work in this book.

1. Will he be home by 9;30.

2. I bet you caught one mistake in line 1? Did you find mistake number 2.

3. I don't think I would like to use a tpyewriter erasure.

4. It is very important to proofread carefully.

5. Will he be in on the 19ht?

6. I wonder what coretcion he will come up with nxet.

7. Now, I wil check my work.

Evaluation

Your work should look like this:

1. Will he be home by 9;30.

2. I bet you caught one mistake in line 1? Did you find mistake number 2.

3. I don't think I would like to use a tpyewriter erasure.

4. It is very important to proofread carefully.

5. Will he be in on the 19ht?

6. I wonder what corretcion he will come up with nxet.

7. Now, I wil check my work.

   Did you miss more than one mistake? If so, be much more careful when you proofread. If you found all of the mistakes that's great! You are ready to take the Self-Test.

SELF-TEST

This Self-Test will help you determine how well you have met the objectives for this chapter and whether you are ready to go on to the next chapter. An evaluation guide follows.

1. Type the names and abbreviations below. Be sure to use the four steps in typing capitals (page 59–60). Come back to the home keys before you type each new stroke. Check the Self-Test Evaluation to see how well you did.

    ```
    IRS
    TWA
    Fourth Street
    Jasper Gray
    East Third Street
    ```

2. (a) If you have a pica (85) machine, set your left margin at 12 and set the tab on your machine to stop at the usual place for indenting. After you set the tab, press the tabulator key. Where should your machine stop?

    (b) If you have elite (102) type on your machine, set the left margin at 21 and indent to the usual place. After you have done this, press the tabulator key. Where should your machine stop?

3. Read the following sentences carefully. Circle any mistakes. There may be sentences where no correction is needed.

    (a) He came much to late to help us.

    (b) Where are you going.

    (c) He comes from Deleware.

    (d) She stop the car.

    (e) Their will be no meetnig on Tuwsday.

    (f) Will you be able to come.

    (g) He live on Fourth Street.

    (h) Please come over.

    (i) Can you find the mistake in this sentence.

    (j) This is the bedt time to come over.

    After you have identified the mistakes, type the sentences correctly. Single space. Proofread your paper while it is still in the machine, and make neat corrections.

Evaluation Guide

Compare your work on the Self-Test to the material given below. The numbers in parentheses refer to the page numbers where the answers can be found. If you have a mistake or are not altogether sure about some material, review those pages before you go on to the next chapter.

1. Did you come back into home position before typing each new capital letter? For example, in IRS, you should have typed the I using the left hand on the shift key, returned to home position, typed the R with the right hand on the shift key, returned to home position, and typed the S with the right hand on the shift key. (pages 57–60)

    If you did everything right, great. If you didn't, repeat the exercise until you type everything properly. Proofread your work carefully and make neat corrections. You can go on if you had less than two "flying capitals." If you had more "flying capitals" type all the names again.

2. (a) Your machine should stop at space 17. (page 61–62)

    (b) Your machine should stop at space 26. (page 61–62)

3. Your circled mistakes should look like this:

    (a) He came much(to)late to help us.

    (b) Where are you going⌢

    (c) He comes from(Deleware)

    (d) She(stop)the car.

    (e) (Their)will be no(meetnig)on(Tuwsday).

    (f) Will you be able to come⌢

    (g) He(live)on Fourth Street.

    (h) Please come over.

    (i) Can you find the mistake in this sentence⌢

    (j) This is the(bedt)time to come over.

    Your typed paper should look like this (if you didn't type the letters in parentheses, that's okay):

    ```
    (a)   He came much too late to help us.
    (b)   Where are you going?
    (c)   He comes from Delaware.
    (d)   She stopped (or stops) the car.
    (e)   There will be no meeting on Tuesday.
    ```

```
(f)   Will you be able to come?
(g)   He lives (or lived) on Fourth Street.
(h)   Please come over.
(i)   Can you find the mistake in this sentence?
(j)   This is the best time to come over.
```

There were eleven mistakes. If you found nine or more of them before you started typing and corrected all eleven of them when you typed, you are ready to move ahead. Let's look, however, at the types of mistakes to determine if you are missing any particular type.

Mistakes in word choice: in sentence (a), "to" is the wrong word. The correct word is "too." In sentence (e), "their" is the wrong word. The correct word is "there."

Mistake in spelling: in sentence (c), "Deleware" is incorrect. The correct spelling is "Delaware."

Mistakes in grammar: in sentence (d), "stop" should be "stopped" or "stops." In sentence (g), "live" should be "lives" or "lived."

Mistakes in punctuation, especially failing to use the question mark: sentence (b), (f), and (i) should end with question marks.

Typing mistakes (inverted letters and wrong keys): in sentence (e) "meetnig" should be "meeting" and "Tuwsday" should be "Tuesday," In sentence (j), "bedt" should be "best." (pages 63-65)

The best typists make mistakes. The important thing is that the mistakes are located and corrected. If you missed particular types of mistakes, look for them very carefully when you type. If you missed finding more than two mistakes, review the material on proofreading in this chapter and try to locate the mistakes in the examples once more before you move ahead to Chapter 6.

CHAPTER SIX

Numbers and Other Symbols

In this first part of this chapter, you will learn to type numbers. Then you will learn other symbols on the keyboard, starting with the : (colon), ? (question mark), and the ½ and ¼ keys. These keys are the same locations on all typewriters. You will also learn to type other fractions, which are typed the same way on most typewriters. Then, there will be a section on other symbol keys common to electric typewriters: the - (dash), the _ (underline), the ' (apostrophe), '' (quotation mark), the = (equal sign), and the + (addition sign) keys.

Next you will learn to type the keys common to the manual machines: the ¢ (cents sign), the @ ("at" sign), and the * (asterisk). A brief outline of the symbols on the *number row*, *upper case* on various types of machines will also be presented.

For your work in this chapter, you will need a typewriter and about 15 sheets of standard-size typing paper. You will also need your choice of material to make corrections.

OBJECTIVE

After completing this chapter, you will be able to:

- type a paragraph five lines long that uses many of the numbers and other symbols covered in the chapter, with no more than two uncorrected mistakes.

Numbers are much easier to learn than letters because they are in order. Many typists type numbers only in addresses, dates, occasional lists, phone numbers and page numbers. If you expect to type numbers often, it is important that you learn to type them with good technique. However, if you do not plan to type numbers often, you may look at the number row on the keyboard when you type a number. Don't let this lead you into a bad habit of looking at letter keys, however. Even if you do look, you should use the correct fingers to type the number keys. When you type a phone number, a ZIP code, a date, or other series of six or eight numbers in a row, you may hold your fingers over the number row and use the number row as your "home row." This is the *only* time you should leave the home row!

NUMBER ROW, LEFT HAND: 1, 2, 3, 4, 5

Remember, to *strike* the keys on the number row. Don't push them. If you have a manual machine, be sure to *strike* the number keys *with the same amount of force* you use for the letter keys. On all machines, be sure to type the number keys with your *fingers;* do not work with your arms, elbows, and/or shoulders. Be especially careful not to brush against other keys when you type numbers.

Look now at Figure 6-1. You see that the 1, 2, 3, 4, and 5 keys are typed with the fingers on your left hand. If your typewriter does not have a 1 key, type the lower case (small, *not* capital) of the letter L on the home row. The illustration also shows the correct fingers to use for the 1, 2, 3, 4, and 5 keys.

Figure 6-1   Number Row, Left Hand: 1, 2, 3, 4, 5

Note: as you learn the numbers 1, 2, 3, 4, and 5, you will type each number only five times. After you have covered all the numbers through 5, there will be practice with all of the numbers on the left hand.

The 1 Key

Check your machine. If you do not have a 1 key on the numbers row, skip to the number 2 key. If you do have a 1 key, look at Figure 6-2. You should type the 1 key with your A finger. Keep at least your F finger anchored in place so that if your other fingers move, they will snap back into place.

Figure 6-2   The 1 Key

Type five 1's and move to the 2 key, below.

The 2 Key

Strike the 2 and all number keys. Don't push them. As you see in Figure 6-3 you type the 2 with your S finger. You will probably have to move all of your other fingers except the F finger when you type the 2. Type five 2's and then go on to the 3 key.

Figure 6-3   The 2 Key

The 3 Key

Figure 6-4 shows that you type the 3 with your D finger. Again make sure your finger, not your shoulder, arm, or elbow does the work. If you leave the home keys with your other fingers, be sure to keep the F finger anchored in place. Now, type five 3's, and then move to the 4 key.

Figure 6-4   The 3 Key

The 4 Key

Strike the 4 with your F finger. Keep your A *finger anchored* in place. Be careful not to brush against other keys if you raise your S and D fingers. Look at Figure 6-5. Type five 4's, and then go on to the 5 key.

Figure 6-5   The 4 Key

The 5 Key

When you type the 5, do your best to let just your F finger do the work. Again, keep your A finger anchored in place and be careful not to brush against other keys if your other fingers leave the home row. Look at Figure 6-6. Type five 5's. Then you will have a chance to apply everything you have learned about numbers up to this point.

Figure 6-6   The 5 Key

Application

You will now have an opportunity to type numbers on the left side of the number row. Be sure to use the correct fingers and to keep either your F finger or your A finger in place on the home row. Try to strike the keys with your fingers. Do your best not to move your arm, elbow, or shoulder. Type the number keys with the same amount of force as you use to strike the other keys.

You will also be typing capital letters. Be sure to use the shift key on the opposite hand and to follow the four steps in typing capitals, pages 59-60. Leave two spaces after *all* periods in the material. Type the following material all the way through. Do *not* stop to make corrections until you have typed the entire exercise. Do not get discouraged if you make mistakes. After you type all of the material, proofread your work and make neat corrections *before* you take the paper out of your machine.

Type each line four times. Type the line number and a period on the left, then space two times before you start typing the line. Single space repeated material, but double space before you type a new line for the first time. If you have questions about the format, glance at the Evaluation on the next page.

From this point until you are instructed otherwise, set your margins at 16 and 91 for elite type and at 7 and 82 for pica type.

Now, you are ready to type.

1.   Our children are 4, 3, and 1.   The youngest was born in 1979.

2.   He sent me model number 143.   I ordered number 134.

3.   We will take Coastal Airlines Flight 414.   He will be on 235.

4.   He is down to 215 pounds from 221.   He has to reach 155.

Evaluation

Your paper should look like this:

```
1.  Our children are 4, 3, and 1.  The youngest was born in 1979.
1.  Our children are 4, 3, and 1.  The youngest was born in 1979.
1.  Our children are 4, 3, and 1.  The youngest was born in 1979.
1.  Our children are 4, 3, and 1.  The youngest was born in 1979.

2.  He sent me model number 143.  I ordered number 134.
2.  He sent me model number 143.  I ordered number 134.
2.  He sent me model number 143.  I ordered number 134.
2.  He sent me model number 143.  I ordered number 134.

3.  We will take Coastal Airlines Flight 414.  He will be on 235.
3.  We will take Coastal Airlines Flight 414.  He will be on 235.
3.  We will take Coastal Airlines Flight 414.  He will be on 235.
3.  We will take Coastal Airlines Flight 414.  He will be on 235.

4.  He is down to 215 pounds from 221.  He has to reach 155.
4.  He is down to 215 pounds from 221.  He has to reach 155.
4.  He is down to 215 pounds from 221.  He has to reach 155.
4.  He is down to 215 pounds from 221.  He has to reach 155.
```

Now, *proofread* very carefully what you have typed. Do not take the paper out of your machine until you have made neat corrections. Count the number of mistakes. Did you type most of the right numbers? Did you avoid "skipping" and light and dark strokes?

If you made such mistakes, make sure to *strike* the number keys. Don't push them. Also, be sure to use the same amount of force in typing numbers as you use in typing letters.

How did your capital letters turn out? If you had "flying capitals," you probably did not complete one step before you started another. Did you remember to space twice after all periods?

If you made seven mistakes or fewer *before* you made corrections, you did very well. (Remember that you typed 16 lines.) You are ready to learn to type the Number Row, Right Hand.

If you made more than seven mistakes, determine the keys where you made more than two mistakes. Practice typing those keys using correct stroking and good technique. Use the Table of Contents to find the page number of the appropriate material. Then type the material again before going on.

NUMBER ROW, RIGHT HAND: 6, 7, 8, 9, 0 (ZERO)

In Figure 6-7, you can see that the numbers 6, 7, 8, 9, and 0 are typed with the right hand. You also see the fingers you use to type them. (The other keys on the top row will be discussed later in the chapter.)

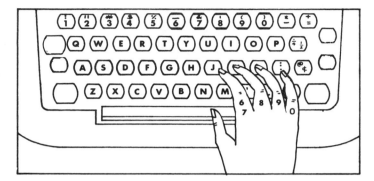

Figure 6-7   Number Row, Right Hand: 6, 7, 8, 9, 0 (Zero)

Remember to strike each key as if it were hot. Don't push the keys. If you have a manual machine, remember to strike each number with the same amount of force you use to type the letters. Now, let's study each key individually.

The 6 Key

Type the 6 with the J finger. This is the longest reach on the keyboard. Keep your ; finger anchored in place. Don't let any of your fingers brush against other keys. Look at Figure 6-8. Then type five 6's, and move ahead to the 7 key.

Figure 6-8   The 6 Key

The 7 Key

Type the 7 with your J finger. Keep at least your ; finger anchored in place.
Look at Figure 6-9. Type five 7's, and then go on to the 8 key.

Figure 6-9   The 7 Key

The 8 Key

Type the 8 with your K finger. Keep at least the ; finger in place, as shown
in Figure 6-10. Type five 8's, and go on to the 9 key.

Figure 6-10   The 8 Key

The 9 Key

Type the 9 with your L finger. Keep the J finger in place. Try your best to
move your arm, elbow, and shoulder as little as possible. Let your finger do
the work. Be careful not to brush against other keys as your fingers leave the
home row. The 9 is a difficult reach. If you have a manual machine, make
sure you use the *same amount of force* as you use for other keys. Look at
Figure 6-11 to see how to type the 9.

Figure 6-11   The 9 Key

Type five 9's, and then move to the 0 (zero) key.

The 0 (Zero) Key

There are two ways to type zero. You may type the capital letter "O" or the zero on the number row. (On a computer terminal, however, you must use the zero key for the number zero.) If you use the zero on the number row, strike it with your ; finger, keeping your J finger anchored in place. Make sure your other fingers do not brush against other keys as they leave the home row.

Now, type the *zero* on the *number row* five times. Then *backspace* five times, and type the capital letter "O" five times over the same places. (Both keys should look the same.) After you've done this, you're ready to do the following Application.

Application

Here, you will have a chance to type *all* of the numbers you have learned in this chapter. Remember to keep at least one finger anchored in place on the home row when you type any number. Remember to use the same amount of force as you use for letters on every number key. You will also have a chance to type capital letters. Be sure to type the capitals correctly, using the proper fingers for the shift key and to type the letter. Also, remember to leave two spaces after punctuation at the end of a sentence.

Type each line below four times. Type the line number, the period, and add two spaces before typing each sentence. Use the same format you used in the previous Application. After you complete typing the material, leave your paper in your machine until you make corrections.

Now, you are ready to type.

```
1.  They were married in 1977 or 1978.  That seems long ago.

2.  The bus will stop at the terminal at 2300 Fenton Street.

3.  The plane flew at about 600 miles per hour at 37,00 feet.

4.  The speed limit on Route 270 is 55 miles per hour.
```

Evaluation

Your paper should look like this:

```
1.  They were married in 1977 or 1978.  That seems long ago.
1.  They were married in 1977 or 1978.  That seems long ago.
1.  They were married in 1977 or 1978.  That seems long ago.
1.  They were married in 1977 or 1978.  That seems long ago.

2.  The bus will stop at the terminal at 2300 Fenton Street.
2.  The bus will stop at the terminal at 2300 Fenton Street.
2.  The bus will stop at the terminal at 2300 Fenton Street.
2.  The bus will stop at the terminal at 2300 Fenton Street.

3.  The plane flew at about 600 miles per hour at 37,000 feet.
3.  The plane flew at about 600 miles per hour at 37,000 feet.
3.  The plane flew at about 600 miles per hour at 37,000 feet.
3.  The plane flew at about 600 miles per hour at 37,000 feet.

4.  The speed limit on Route 270 is 55 miles per hour.
4.  The speed limit on Route 270 is 55 miles per hour.
4.  The speed limit on Route 270 is 55 miles per hour.
4.  The speed limit on Route 270 is 55 miles per hour.
```

Proofread carefully what you just typed. Do not take your paper out of your typewriter until you have corrected all mistakes neatly. Count the number of corrections you make.

☆ Did you type the correct numbers?

☆ Were all of your strokes the same shade?

☆ Was there any "skipping"?

☆ Did your capital letters come out right?

☆ Did you space twice after each period?

If you made seven mistakes or fewer *before* you made corrections, you did very well. You are ready to move ahead. If you made more than seven mistakes, determine the keys on which you made more than two mistakes. Practice those keys using correct stroking and good technique.

Use the Table of Contents to find the page number of the appropriate material. After you retype the material, you will be ready to move ahead to the next section.

OTHER SYMBOLS

The symbols on the upper case of the numbers row will be discussed later. Now, let's tie together loose ends by covering the remainder of the keys on the three letter rows. First you will learn about keys common to all typewriters. Then there will be a section on keys common to electric typewriters and a section on the keys common to manual (non-electric) typewriters.

The location of special symbols on computer terminals varies widely with the makes and models of computers. Check the manual for the computer you have as you look at the keyboard on your computer.

Symbol Keys Common to All Typewriters: : (Colon), ? (Question Mark), ½ (One-Half), ¼ (One-Fourth), Other Fractions

Figure 6-12 shows the : (colon), the ? (question mark), the ½ (one-half) and the ¼ (one-fourth) keys. You will use the ; (semi) finger to type all of these keys.

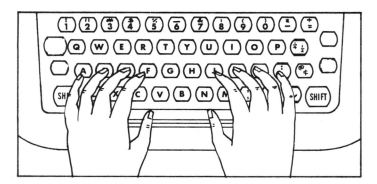

Figure 6-12 The Colon, Question Mark, One-Half, One-Fourth Keys

The Colon Key

Figure 6-13 shows you that the : (colon) key is the *upper case* or "capital" of the ; key. (The term "upper case" refers to the character typed when the shift key is depressed.) Use the A finger to depress the *shift key* and do your best to move only your ; finger when you type the :. Be sure to use the same amount of force on the : as you use on your other keys. (In typing the : key you use the weakest fingers on both hands.) Type five : 's, and then move to the (question mark) key.

Figure 6-13   The : (Colon) Key

The Question Mark Key

Figure 6-14 shows you that the ? (question mark) key is the upper case or "capital" of the / (slash) key. Type it with your ; finger. Try to keep your other fingers in place. If your L finger and/or other fingers move, be sure to return them to home position before you type a new key. Type five ?'s and go on to the ½ key.

Figure 6-14   The ? (Question Mark) Key

The One-Half Key

The ½ (one-half) key is next to the P key. You should be able to type the ½ key by moving your ; finger only. Look at Figure 6-15. Type five ½'s, and then move to the ¼ key.

Figure 6-15   The ½ (One-Half) Key

The One-Fourth Key

The ¼ (one-fourth) key is the upper case, or "capital" of the ½ key. Use the
; finger to type the ¼. Depress the left shift key with your A finger. Look
at the illustration, type five ¼'s, and then move ahead.

Figure 6-16   The ¼ (One-Fourth) Key

Typing Other Fractions

You will use the / (slash mark) to type other fractions. If you want to type
the fraction one-third, simply type the l, type the /, and then type the three.
The fraction will look like this: 1/3.

To type four-fifths, type the 4, type the /, and type the 5. Your fraction will look like this: 4/5.

If you are typing ½ and/or ¼ along with other fractions, you might
want to use the slash mark in typing 1/2 and 1/4 so the fractions will be
uniform throughout.

Application

Type each of the following lines three times. Single space repeated material, and double space before you type a new line for the first time. This material is very difficult. You will be asked to type it only one time through, even if you make many mistakes. Do *not* get discouraged if you make a lot of mistakes.

```
1.   His temperature is 98.6.  His blood pressure is 120/80.

2.   I need size 6 7/8, 7, or 7 1/8.  What size do you wear?

3.   Registration starts at 8:30.  The meeting begins at 9:00.

4.   Our children are 6½ and 8½.  How old are your children?

5.   I paid 1/7.  He paid 2/7.  Together we paid 3/7.
```

Evaluation

Your paper should look like this:

```
1.   His temperature is 98.6.  His blood pressure is 120/80.
1.   His temperature is 98.6.  His blood pressure is 120/80.
1.   His temperature is 98.6.  His blood pressure is 120/80.

2.   I need size 6 7/8, 7, or 7 1/8.  What size do you wear?
2.   I need size 6 7/8, 7, or 7 1/8.  What size do you wear?
2.   I need size 6 7/8, 7, or 7 1/8.  What size do you wear?

3.   Registration starts at 8:30.  The meeting begins at 9:00.
3.   Registration starts at 8:30.  The meeting begins at 9:00.
3.   Registration starts at 8:30.  The meeting begins at 9:00.

4.   Our children are 6½ and 8½.  How old are your children?
4.   Our children are 6½ and 8½.  How old are your children?
4.   Our children are 6½ and 8½.  How old are your children?

5.   I paid 1/7.  He paid 2/7.  Together we paid 3/7.
5.   I paid 1/7.  He paid 2/7.  Together we paid 3/7.
5.   I paid 1/7.  He paid 2/7.  Together we paid 3/7.
```

Leave your paper in your machine. Proofread carefully to find all mistakes. Correcting your mistakes is optional here. It is important, however, to find them.

You don't have to retype any of the material above, unless you want to. If you are interested in symbols on electric typewriters, read the next section. If you want to learn about the symbols on manual machines, skip ahead to that section.

Other Symbols on Electric Typewriters : – (Dash), _ (Underline),
" (Quotation Mark), ' (Apostrophe), = (Equal Sign), + (Addition)

Now, you will learn to type the – (dash), the _ (underline), " (quotation mark), ' (apostrophe), = (equal sign), and the + (addition) on electric type-writers. Look at Figure 6-17 to learn the locations of these keys. Again, you will type all of these keys with your ; finger.

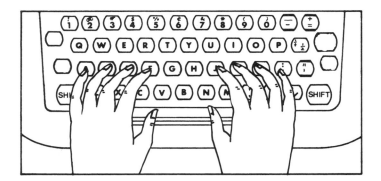

Figure 6-17   Other Symbols on Electric Typewriters: – (Dash), _ (Underline),
" (Quotation Mark), ' (Apostrophe), = (Equal Sign), + (Addition
Sign)

The Dash Key

Use the ; finger to type the – (dash) key. Be sure to keep at least your J finger anchored in place.

Figure 6-18   The – (Dash) Key

On some electric typewriters, the – is a *continuous* key, which means it repeats as long as you hold it down. If you have a continuous key and want to type only one – , be careful to *strike* the key from above as if it were hot. Do *not* push or "lean on" the – key. Type five – 's, and move on.

The Underline Key

The _ (underline) key is the upper case or "capital" of the dash key. If your dash key is continuous, your underline key is too. You type the underline key with your two weakest fingers. Be sure to keep both your J and F fingers anchored in place. Type the underline key five times, and then move on to the apostrophe key below.

Figure 6-19   The _ (Underline) Key

The Apostrophe Key

The ' (apostrophe) key is just to the right of the ; key. Type it with the ; finger. Type five apostrophes and move ahead.

Figure 6-20   The ' (Apostrophe) Key

The Quotation Mark Key

The " (quotation mark) key is the upper case of the ' key. Use the shift key on your left hand. Be sure to anchor your F finger in place. You should type the " with the ; finger. Look at Figure 6-21, type five quotation marks, and move on to the equal sign key.

Figure 6-21   The " (Quotation Mark) Key

The Equal Sign Key

The = (equal sign) key is just to the right of the dash key. Type it with your
; finger. Keep at least your J finger anchored in place. Be very careful not to
brush against other keys when you reach for the =. Look at Figure 6-22, type
five = 's, and move ahead.

Figure 6-22   The = (Equal Sign) Key

The Addition Sign Key

The + (addition sign) key is the upper case of the = key. Use the shift key on
your left hand. Then type the + key the same way you typed the = key. Be
sure to keep at least your F and J fingers in place, and be careful not to
brush against other keys. Look at Figure 6-23, and then type five + 's.

Figure 6-23   The + (Addition) Key

If you want to learn about the special keys on manual typewriters, continue with the next section. Otherwise, skip ahead to the section, "Number Row, Upper Case."

Other Symbols on Manual Typewriters: ¢ (Cents), @ (At), * (Asterisk)

This section will cover the ¢ (cents) key, the @ (at) key, and the * (asterisk) key. Figure 6-24 shows the position of these keys on the keyboard.

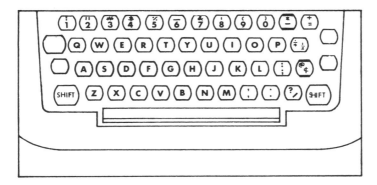

Figure 6-24   The @ (At), ¢ (Cents), and * (Asterisk) Keys

The Cents Key

The ¢ (cents) key is just to the right of the ; key. Move your ; finger only when you type the ¢ key. Be sure to type it with the same amount of force as you use other keys. Look at Figure 6-25, then type the ¢ key five times before you move ahead.

Figure 6-25   The ¢ (Cents) Key

The At Key

The @ (at) key is the upper case of the ¢ key. Use the shift key on the left hand side of your machine. Be sure to keep your F finger anchored in place. Then type the @ key with your ; finger. Be sure you use enough force to avoid light and dark shading. Look at Figure 6-26, type the @ key five times, and then move to the next section

Figure 6-26   The @ (At) Key

The Asterisk Key

The * (asterisk) is the upper case of the underline key. You will type the * with your two weakest fingers. Be sure to apply enough force so that the * will be the same shade as your other keys. Remember to use the shift key on your left hand. Anchor your F finger in place. Type the * with the ; finger. Do your best to let your *finger* do most of the work. Be careful not to brush against other keys as your fingers move toward the top row. Look at Figure 6-27, then type five * 's before you move to the next section.

Figure 6-27   The * (Asterisk) Key

SYMBOLS ON NUMBER ROW

The upper case keys on the numbers row are not frequently used. Therefore, there will be lists of upper case numbers keys common to all machines, of those common to electric typewriters, and of those common to manual machines. If you wish, you may practice on these keys, but you are not required to do so.

Keys Common to All Machines: (#, $, %, &, (,))

The upper case of the 3 key is #. It means number or pound.

The upper case of the 4 key is $. It, of course, is the dollar sign.

The upper case of the 5 key is %. It means, "percent."

The upper case of the 7 key is &. It is the ampersand. It means "and."

The upper case of the 9 key is (. It is called "open parentheses."

The upper case of the 0 (zero) key is). It is called "close parentheses."

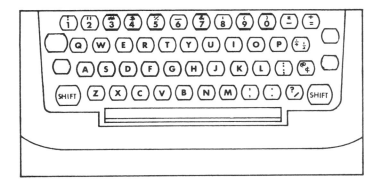

Figure 6-28   Number Row, Upper Case on All Machines: #, $, %, &, (,)

Keys on Electric Machines Only

The upper case of the 2 key is @. It means "at."

The upper case of the 6 key is ¢. It means "cents."

The upper case of the 8 key is *. It is the asterisk.

Keys on Manual Machines Only

The upper case of the 2 key is ". It is used to *open* and *close* quotations.

The upper case of the 6 key is _. It is used to underline.

The upper case of the 8 key is '. It is the apostrophe.

Now it is time for your self-test.

Application (Optional)

The new keys in this application are used far less frequently than the keys learned up to this point. For that reason, this application exercise is optional. Type the paragraph below. Double space.

```
     The @ means "at."   The # means "number or pound."  The

$, which is the upper case or "capital" 4, is of course,

the dollar sign.  % means "percent."  ¢ means, of course, "

"cents."  & means "and," of course.  The * is the asterisk.

The symbol (is used to open parentheses and the ) is used to

close them.  The _ is used to underline and the - is the

dash.  The fraction "one-half" is written ½, and ¼ is the

fraction "one-quarter."  The ' is the apostrophe.

     I am now finished with this @, #, $, %, ¢, &, *, (, ),

_, -, =, ½, ¼ exercise.
```

Evaluation

How did you do? Does your paper look anything like the material above? If it does, that's great. If not, remember that this exercise was optional, and that you probably will not use these keys very often.

Now it is time for your Self-Test.

SELF-TEST

This Self-Test will help you determine how well you have met the objective for this chapter and whether you are ready to go on to the next chapter. An Evaluation guide follows.

Type the paragraph below all the way through, double spaced. Then proofread carefully for mistakes and correct neatly. Indent, punctuate, and capitalize exactly as shown in the paragraph. When you complete the paragraph, do *not* remove the paper from your machine.

```
     I was doing well in this typing course.  But, I'll never

have to type fractions like 1/3 or 4/5 anyway.  If I get

hung up on the ;, ', " keys, I'll still be taking this

course weeks from now.  I guess, I'll just keep plugging

away.  What's in store next?  I will see soon.
```

Evaluation Guide

Compare your work on the Self-Test to the guidelines given below. The numbers in parentheses refer to the chapters where appropriate material can be found. If you have a mistake or are not sure about something, review the material before you go on to the next chapter.

You might also have someone else check for mistakes. Correct your mistakes.

☆ Did you indent correctly? (Chapter 5)

☆ Did you have flying capitals? (Chapter 5)

☆ Did you miss some letters? (Chapters 2, 3, 4)

☆ Did you have trouble with numbers or symbols? (Chapter 6)

☆ Did you have messy corrections? (Chapter 5)

If you have no more than two uncorrected and/or messy corrections, you are ready to move ahead to the next chapter, where you will see how fast you can type. If you made more than two uncorrected and/or messy mistakes, repeat the Self-Test before you move ahead.

CHAPTER SEVEN

Timed Typings

In this chapter, you will first learn to take one-minute timed writings and the way to compute your speed. The third one-minute timing will serve as the Self-Test for this chapter. As an optional exercise, you will have a chance to take three five-minute timings and compute your speed.

For this chapter you will need a timer that buzzes or rings when the time is up, a typewriter, and several sheets of standard-size paper.

OBJECTIVES

After completing this chapter you will be able to:

- type for one minute at a steady pace with two mistakes or fewer; and

- type for five minutes at a steady pace with no more than seven mistakes. (optional)

You should take the three one-minute timings in this chapter even if you will not have to take a typing test. The timings will tell you how fast you can type and how well you perform at the typewriter under moderate pressure.

If you are going to take a timed typing test, you should take all of the timings in this chapter as well as those in Appendix A. You may want to practice by taking each of the five-minute timings several times.

A note about typing tests: in the past, deductions were made from typing speed for mistakes. Today this is rarely done. Instead, you are likely to be given two scores, one for speed and the other for accuracy. For example, if you type 20 words per minute with 7 mistakes, your score will probably be recorded as 20/7. No deduction will be made from the 20 words per minute for the seven errors. Most employment tests for typists are for five minutes.

When you compute speed, each five strokes (including spaces) counts as one word. This compensates for long and short words.

GENERAL INSTRUCTIONS

If you have pica (85) type, set your margins at 7 and 82. If you are using a machine with elite (102) type, set your margins at 16 and 91.

When you take a timed writing *always make sure you have space on your paper to complete the timing.* After a little experience, you will know how much space you need to type a timed writing. At first, it is probably best to start each new timing on a clean side of paper.

ONE-MINUTE TIMINGS

In the first examples, you will indent new paragraphs. Set your line space regulator to double space. Remember to space twice after a period at the end of a sentence. Keep your eyes on the material you are typing from. Try to remember to start and end each line exactly where it starts and ends in the book. Do not stop typing before time is up even if you have made several mistakes. If you complete the material before time is up, start typing it a second time. The numbers on the right side of the page and those at the bottom will help you compute your speed (as will be explained). *Do not type the numbers.*

First One-Minute Timing

Set your timer for one minute. Then type the following material until your time is up.

```
    I have learned the typewriter keyboard and I want to see        11

how fast I can type.  I wonder what my speed will be.               23

----1----2----3----4----5----6----7----8----9---10---11---12---13
```

Check your paper for mistakes. If you made two mistakes or fewer, you are ready to compute your speed. If you made more than two mistakes, correct your errors and take the timing again. After you take it a second time, you may compute your speed. Then move to the second one-minute timing regardless of the number of mistakes you made.

How to Compute Speed for One-Minute Timings

1. Find the number at the end of the last complete line you typed. For example, if you typed through the word "fast" on the second line, the number at the end of your last complete line is 11.

2. Locate the number on the bottom closest to the word where you stopped typing. For example, if you typed through "fast" the number on the bottom line nearest to that word is 2.

3. Add both numbers together. This is your typing speed. In this example you should add 11 and 2, giving you a speed of 13 words per minute.

4. If you typed the entire paragraph once and then typed part of it a second time, add 23 to your score to give yourself credit for typing the entire paragraph once. If you typed the paragraph once and got to "fast" on the second line again, add 23 and 13, giving you a speed of 36 words per minute.

Second One-Minute Timing

Set your timer for one minute. Then type the following material until your time is up.

```
     Most people write in longhand at speeds of twenty to        10

thirty words per minute.  A few people can write at speeds in    22

the low and mid thirties.  For most typing jobs, a typing speed  34

of forty words per minute or faster is required.                 44
----1----2----3----4----5----6--+-7----8----9---10---11---12
```

If you made two mistakes or fewer, terrific. Compute your speed. If you made more than two mistakes, correct the mistakes you made and type the material a second time. After you have typed the material a second time, move to the third one-minute timing below. The third timing serves as your Self-Test.

Third One-Minute Timing

Set your timer for one minute and type the following material until your time is up.

```
     You probably learned in government or political science class that  13

each state elects two members to the U. S. Senate, regardless of its    27

population.                                                             29
----1----2----3----4----5----6----7----8----9---10---11---13---14
```

If you made two mistakes or fewer, that's tremendous. You may either move to the optional timings that follow, or the ones in Appendix A, or go on to Chapter 8.

If you made more than two mistakes, determine the key or keys on which you made one or more mistakes. Refer to the Table of Contents to locate the appropriate material you need to review. Then, if you wish, take the optional timings. If you do not take these timings, move to the next chapter on typing reports.

FIVE-MINUTE TIMINGS (OPTIONAL)

Follow the same instructions as you did for the one-minute timings, except do not indent. The instructions appear on page 95. Do not stop typing before time is up even if you have made mistakes. Now, you are ready to type.

First Five-Minute Timing

Set your timer for five minutes and type the following material until your time is up.

```
Our research has shown that several patents in your area of          2

interest have been issued in recent years.  There are also          5

several articles which have appeared in the journals.  As a          7

patent can be issued only for a new invention, it would seem          9

to us that you would not be able to claim patent rights unless,      11

of course, you come up with a completely new development of          14

which there are no previous descriptions or articles.  We           16

would suggest that you do not go to the work or expense of           19

filing a claim for a patent at this time.  Of course, if            21

you decide to go ahead, we will be happy to represent you.          24
------------------------1--------------------2------------------------
```

Leave your paper in the machine. Check it carefully. If you made seven mistakes or fewer, that's tremendous. Correct your mistakes neatly and compute your speed (see the instructions below). Now, go on to the next timing.

If you made more than seven mistakes, that's still pretty good, since this was the first chance you have had to type for five minutes. Correct your mistakes. Then take the timing again. After the second time, you may compute your speed.

How To Compute Speed For Five-Minute Timings

Basically, you compute your speed for five-minute timings the same way you did for the one-minute timings. However, the *numbers* on the right side of the exercise and at the bottom have been adjusted, and these should be used *only for five minute timings.*

Follow these steps:

1. Find the number at the end of the last full line you typed in the first five-minute timing. Let's assume that you typed through "articles" four lines from the bottom of the timing. The number at the end of the last complete line is 14.

2. Find the number at the bottom of the page closest to the point you stopped typing. In this example, the number is 2.

3. Add the two numbers. In this example, you would add 14 and 2, and you would have typed at a speed of 16 words per minute.

4. If you typed the entire passage and began typing it a second time, add 24 words per minute to your score to give yourself credit for the first time you typed the material. If you got through "articles" the second time around, you would add 24 and 16 and would have typed at a speed of 40 words per minute.

Second Five-Minute Timing

Set your timer for five minutes and type from the following material until your time is up.

```
Thank you for your recent letter.  We would have answered it        2

earlier, but Bob was away for two weeks to take care of some        5

problems in our Western Region.  Our supervisors there have         7

to get more work of their employees, which will be difficult       10

because they must also maintain good relations with our rank       12

and file employees.

I will pass on the suggestions you made in your letter to our      15

Board of Directors and will suggest that they adopt your plan      18

and act as quickly as possible.                                    19
------------------------1-------------------------2--------------
```

If you made seven mistakes or fewer, that's great. You may compute your speed and move on to the next timing. If you made more than seven mistakes, type the material again. Compute your speed on the second typing, then move to the third timing regardless of the number of mistakes you make.

Third Five-Minute Timing

Set your timer for five minutes and type from the following material until your time runs out.

```
I have learned the typewriter keyboard in just a few weeks.        2

I can locate every key on the machine that I am using.  I will     5

learn how to type reports, business letters, and tables in         7

the remainder of this book.  I can already type almost as          10

fast as I can write in longhand.  It is a lot easier to read       12

typewritten material than material which is written in             14

longhand.  Since everybody can read my typing, I must be           16

careful not to type what I do not want read.                       17

I wonder how many Self-Teaching Guides Wiley has published.        20

I wonder if the character who wrote this one has written any       22

others.  If he has, should I buy them?  I am sure he could         25

use the money.                                                     26
-------------1-----------------------2-----------------------
```

Check for accuracy before you compute your speed. If you typed with seven mistakes or fewer, correct your mistakes, and then go on to the next chapter.

If you made more than seven mistakes, find the strokes on which you made two or more mistakes. Then practice those keys and retype *any* of the five-minute timings. Locate and correct any mistakes in the retyping before you move ahead. If you are anxious to build typing speed, you may want to take the timings in Appendix A and/or repeat any of the timings in this chapter. You may also want to come back to this chapter again after you have completed the book to determine how much speed you have picked up while learning to type reports, letters, and tables in the following chapters.

CHAPTER EIGHT

Typing Reports

First, in this chapter, you will learn general rules for setting up reports. Then you will have a chance to type three reports. The third report will serve as your Self-Test.

For this chapter, you will need a typewriter, a 12-inch ruler, and several sheets of standard-size typing paper. You will continue to use the ruler in the remaining chapters of this book.

OBJECTIVE

After completing this chapter, you will be able to:

- type a report in the correct format with two or fewer uncorrected mistakes.

Appendix B gives general instructions on setting up a backing sheet which you can place under your paper to guide you in typing reports.

There are many ways to type reports, and there is no one "correct" way. Many schools and organizations have their own style guides. If you have to conform to a particular style, use your style guide instead of the style outlined in this chapter.

SETTING UP YOUR REPORT

Remember that a standard-size sheet of typing paper is 8½ inches across by 11 inches up and down. Use your ruler to measure your paper to make sure it is the right size. On reports, you should leave a top margin of about 1½ inches. Since there are 6 vertical lines per inch, the top margin should be about 9 lines. Insert a clean sheet of paper into your typewriter. Start counting from the point where the paper is just visible under the *cylinder* (or where you can type on the page and not on the cylinder).

Use one of the *cylinder knobs* or the *return* and bring the paper up 9 lines. Then make a light pencil mark. This will show you where your top margin is.

You should leave a bottom margin of about 1 inch, or 6 lines. Insert the paper upside down and make a light pencil mark 6 lines from the bottom of the page. Then, bring the paper up another inch or 6 lines and make another pencil mark. This mark will serve as your warning that you are running out of space on the page. If you *single space* and reach this mark, you know you have 6 lines left within the margin. If you *double space*, you have only 3 lines. Never go below the bottom margin. Also, always type at least two lines at the top of a page, never only a few words or only one line. You may have to leave a page 1 line short to have two full lines on the last page.

Leave side margins of 1½ inches. If you have pica (85) type, set the left margin at space 15. If you have elite (102) type, set it at space 18.

You have probably noticed that as you approach the end of a line across, a bell rings when you have only a few spaces left. It is set to ring at different places on different machines. Experiment with your machine to see where the bell rings. When you hear the bell, you generally complete the word you are typing and *return* the carriage or element carrier. Most of the time, you will stop typing *before* your machine locks at the right margin.

We will assume that on the average you will stop typing ½ inch before the machine locks. For that reason, set the right margin at 1 inch from the edge of the paper.

Now, bring your carriage or element carrier to the end of the paper. If you have pica type, have your *paper guide* set at zero, and are using standard-size paper, your paper ends on the right at space 85. Backspace 10 spaces (1 inch) and set the margin at 75. Make a light mark on your page at that point.

If you have an elite machine, your paper will end at space 102. Backspace 12 spaces (1 inch) and set your right margin at space 90. Then make a light pencil mark at that point.

Take your paper out of the machine. It should have lines in the same proportion as the lines in Figure 8-1.

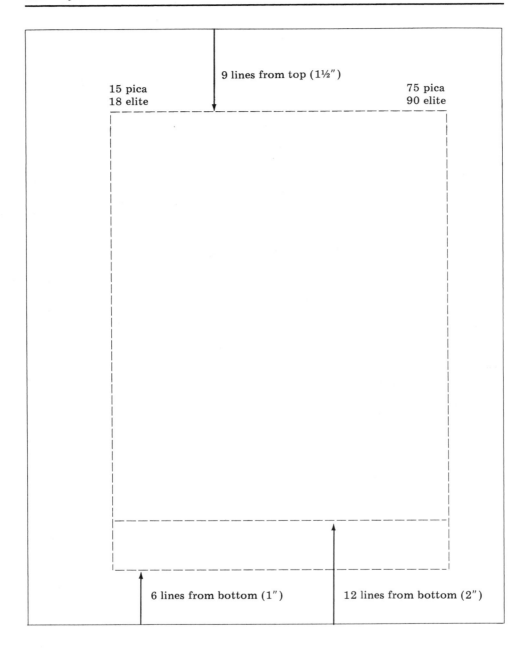

Figure 8-1   Marking Your Paper (shown proportionate to 8½″ x 11″)

Application

With your paper still out of the machine, use your ruler and measure:

1. The space between the top of the page and your pencil mark. How large is the space?

2. The space between the bottom of your page and your stop line on the bottom of the page. How much space do you have?

3. The space between the bottom of the paper and the warning line. How much space do you have there?

4. Measure your left margin. How large is it?

5. Measure your right margin. How much space do you have there?

Evaluation

The correct amount of space is:

1. 1½ inches

2. 1 inch

3. 2 inches

4. 1½ inches

5. 1 inch

How did you do? Did your measurements come out right? If so, that's good. You are ready to move on to the next section on centering titles.

If it didn't come out right, don't be too discouraged. Turn back to page 100 and read the instructions again. Then try marking your paper again.

CENTERING TITLES

Centering titles and other material is simple. Just follow these steps:

1. Count the number of strokes, including spaces and punctuations, in the material to be centered. In the title of this section there are 16 strokes.

    ```
    CENTERING TITLES

    1234567890123456  16
    ```

2. Take half of that number. Half of 16 is 8, If you have a fraction, round off to the lower number.

3. Subtract that number, 8, from the midpoint of your paper and start typing the title at that point. If you have elite type, the midpoint of your

paper is at space 51. If you have pica type, it is at space 42. If you have elite type, you will start typing the title at space 43 (51 minus 8). If your machine has pica type, start typing the title at space 34 (42 minus 8).

Application

Look at this title:

QUICK TYPING

1. At what space would you start typing to center the title if you have elite type?

2. At what space would you start typing it if you have pica type?

3. Type and center the title using the machine you have.

Evaluation

1. The title QUICK TYPING has 12 spaces.

    123456789012

Take half of that number. Half of 12 is 6.
    Subtract 6 from the midpoint of your paper, and start typing at that point.

If you have elite type you will start the title at space 45 (51 minus 6).

2. If you have pica type, you will start it at space 36 (42 minus 6).

3. Does your title appear to be centered? Measure with your ruler the amounts of space on the left of the title and on the right. The amounts should be equal.
    How did you do? Did you get everything right? If so, very good. If you missed any of the steps, turn back to the beginning of the centering material and go through the section and the application again before you type the first report.

REPORTS TO TYPE

First Report

Insert the paper you marked earlier in this chapter. Set your side margins. Make sure they conform to your pencil marks. Indent five spaces for new paragraphs. Double space the body of the report. Your lines will not necessarily start and end where they start and end in this book. When you type, stay within your pencil marks. Center the title. Triple space between the title and the first line of the report. Now, you are ready to type the first report from the following boxed material.

BUSINESS VOCABULARY

There is very little relationship between the most used words in business communication and the words that have special abbreviations or "brief forms" in traditional shorthand. Several studies have shown that ten English words make up about a quarter of all the words used in written business communication. These words are: the, of, to, and, in, you, a, for, we, and your. In James Silverthorn's 1965 study, these words made up 24.67 percent of all words used. Devern Perry found in his 1968 study that these same ten words accounted for 25.71 percent of all the words in his sample.

Many of the most frequently used words do not have special "brief form" abbreviations in traditional short-hand. Even more significant, many words that are rarely used have special abbreviations. As a result, many students become frustrated and "turned off."

This writer feels very strongly that words abbreviated in shorthand should be the same words that are most often used. He has developed a new shorthand system called QUICKHAND. John Wiley & Sons first published QUICKHAND as a Self-Teaching Guide in 1976.

Leave your paper in your machine.

Evaluation

How did you do? Did you stay within the margins? Does your title appear centered? Did you triple space after the title and double space the rest of the report? Proofread your paper carefully and make neat corrections of all of your mistakes.

If you stayed within the margins, that's tremendous. You are ready to move to the second report.

If you went outside the margins, correct your mistakes and type the report again. Make light pencil marks at the appropriate points on your paper before you put it into your typewriter. You should use a ruler to mark off your top and bottom lines. After you type the report again, correct all mistakes before you continue with the second report.

Second Report

Mark your paper as instructed in the first report. You should use a ruler to mark off your top and bottom margins and your bottom warning line.

Do not go beyond the bottom margin. Pay close attention to the bottom warning line. Remember that if you type on a second page, you have to type at least two lines on that page.

Now, type the report from the following boxed material. (Note that the report is continued on page 107.)

CHANGING TIMES

There have been profound changes in technology in recent years. It seems possible that paper money, carbon paper, postage stamps, propellers, arithmetic, railroad tracks, dresses, and clocks with "big hands" and "little hands" might become extinct. Certainly they are on the "endangered species" list.

Along with technology, social enlightenment has made it possible in some cases for women to have jobs that were previously held almost entirely by men. Also, men can have jobs that were previously held mostly by women. Today, women work as corporate officers, newscasters, telephone installers, attorneys, truck drivers, and airline pilots. Many men work as airline flight attendants, secretaries, elementary school teachers, nurses, and telephone operators. (At the turn of the century, most telephone operators were men.)

---

continued

```
        Along with technology, language has also changed.

The term "man" has been replaced in many job titles.

Today, we have police "officers," and "firefighters."

The terms "file clerks" and "typing pools" have

traditionally made most people think of women.  Today,

however, these terms are changing too.  Now, instead

of file clerks, we have "records management

specialists" and instead of typing pools we have

"word processing centers."
```

Leave your paper in your machine.

Evaluation

Did you stay within your lines? Did you triple space after the title and double space the rest of the report? If you did, correct any other mistakes. Then take the Self-Test.

If you went outside the margins, correct your mistakes, and retype the report before you continue with the Self-Test.

In this chapter you've learned about the fundamentals of report typing format. The details of style and format for reports vary widely depending on the subject and situation. For example, a report on a pharmaceutical drug will differ from a college student's history term paper, as the report of a psychological study differs from a research paper in literature. You should refer to the standard style guides for your area or situation.

SELF-TEST

This Self-Test will help you determine how well you have met the objective of this chapter and whether you are ready to go on to the next chapter. An Evaluation guide follows.

Mark off your paper as you have for the first two reports. Follow the same general directions and type your report from the following boxed material.

```
                       NEW PROCEDURES


     In the past, students learned to type on blank key-

boards or with the letters on the keyboard covered.

This was done to encourage students to keep their eyes

on the material they were typing or on a keyboard wall

chart.  However, many students took their eyes off the

material or a wall chart to look up at their papers

to see if they were using the right keys.  For that

reason, students today learn on keyboards that are

marked.

     Before electric typewriters were used, typists

were told to always put the material they were copying

on their right.  It was not placed on the left side,

because the typist would return the carriage with

his left hand and block the line of vision.  However,

with electric typewriters, it is no longer necessary

to keep the material on the right.
```

Leave your paper in the machine.

Evaluation Guide

Proofread your report and neatly correct any mistakes. Then answer the following questions about your report. The numbers in parentheses refer to the chapters (and the page numbers in this chapter) where appropriate review material can be found. If you have a mistake or are not altogether sure about something, review the material in this chapter before you move ahead.

☆ Did you indent correctly? (Chapter 5)

☆ Did you have flying capitals? (Chapter 5)

☆ Did you miss some letters? (Chapters 2, 3, 4)

☆ Did you have trouble with numbers or symbols? (Chapter 6)

☆ Did you have messy corrections? (Chapter 5)

☆ Did you stay within the margins? (Chapter 8 pages 100-102)

☆ Did you triple space after the title and double space the rest of the report? (Chapter 8 page 104)

☆ Did you center the title? (Chapter 8 pages 103-104)

If you had two mistakes or fewer, you are ready to move to the next chapter.

CHAPTER NINE

Typing Letters

In this chapter you will first learn to type letters in the block style. "Block style" means that the main parts of the letter start at the left margin and that paragraphs aren't indented. Then, in optional sections, you will learn how to type letters in modified block styles and how to address envelopes, cards, and labels.

You will need a typewriter, a 12-inch ruler, and about 20 sheets of standard-size typing paper.

If you work in the optional section on envelope, card, and label addressing, you may cut paper into the appropriate sizes and shapes or you may use actual envelopes, cards, and labels. If you use the real envelopes, you will need about five No. 10 envelopes, about five No. 6 3/4 envelopes and about five 3″ by 5″ index file cards. Table 9-2 on page 119 shows the dimensions of these envelopes and cards. Use your ruler to check your materials if you're in doubt.

OBJECTIVE

After completing this chapter you will be able to:

- set up and type a letter in the block style with no uncorrected mistakes.

Note: Appendix C contains instructions on setting up a backing sheet which you may place under your paper and use as a guide. There are also more business letters to type in that appendix.

PARTS OF A BLOCK STYLE LETTER

Figure 9-1 shows the various parts of a block style letter. The following list explains the numbered parts of this letter in Figure 9-1.

(1) Letterhead		**Hippidy Hoppody Press** Briar Patch Lane Bunnyville, New York 10001
(2) Date Line		October 2, 1980
(3) Inside Address		Ms. Susie Zylch 1234 Fifth Street Bethesda, MD 20034
(4) Salutation		Dear Susie:
(5) Body of Letter		This is a short letter typed in the Block Style. Notice that <u>everything</u> typed begins at the left margin.
		The various parts of a letter are defined in this illustration. Study the illustration carefully. Then read the information on the next page.
		As you suggested, I am enclosing a copy of the article I mentioned during our phone call.
(6) Complimentary Close		Sincerely,
(7) Written Signature		*Pete*
(8) Typed Signature		P. Cottentail
(9) Reference initials		PC/me
(10) Enclosure notation		Enc.

Figure 9-1   Parts of The Letter

(1) Most business letters are typed on *letterhead* stationary. The letterhead contains the name and address of the organization that sends the letter. The top margin on the page allows space for the letterhead.

(2) Every letter should be dated. The *date line* is the first line after the letterhead in Figure 9-1. Leave a blank line between the date line and the inside address.

(3) The *inside address* is the address of the person to whom the letter is being sent. Always use an inside address. If the letter should get separated from the envelope, the inside address may help to get the letter delivered to the right office or person.

(4) This is the *salutation*. In a business letter, always use a colon (:) after the salutation, even if you use a first name. In a personal letter, a comma is generally used after the salutation.

(5) The *body* of the letter begins at the left margin in a block style letter. There is no indentation. Leave a blank line between the salutation and the body of the letter. Also, leave a blank line between paragraphs in the body of the letter.

(6) This is the *complimentary close*. Leave a blank line between the end of the body and the complimentary close. Always use a comma in the close.

(7)   Leave three blank lines after the complimentary close for the *written signature.* Today, when people who write know each other, they frequently sign only their first names.

(8)   Every business letter should have a *typewritten signature.* If the person receiving the letter can't read the handwritten signature, the typewritten signature is a big help.

(9)   In a business letter, always type *reference initials* when someone other than the typist is going to sign it. They are generally not used in personal letters. Type the initials of the person who signs the letter in capital letters. Type the slash (/). Then in small letters type the initials of the typist. Leave a blank line between the typed signature and the reference initials.

(10) Indicate enclosed material by "Enc." or "Enclosure" double spaced just below the reference initials. If there are no reference initials, type "Enc." or "Enclosure" two lines below the typed signature.

LETTER PLACEMENT ON TYPEWRITER

The margins on the top and bottom of letters as well as the side margins depend on the length of the letter.

You can usually type about twelve typewritten words on a line. With practice, you will become an expert on "eyeballing" the length of a letter.

Table 9-1 gives you a general idea of how far down on the page you should start and the margins you should use when you type letters.

Table 9-1   Letter Placement Guide

Words in Body	Line Length	Date Line From Top of Page
50 or less	50 spaces	23
51–75	50 spaces	22
76–100	50 spaces	21
101–125	60 spaces	20
126–150	60 spaces	19
151–175	60 spaces	18
176–200	60 spaces	17
201–225	70 spaces	16
226–250	70 spaces	15
251 or more	70 spaces	14

Setting Margins for Line Lengths

If your typewriter has pica (85) type:

  ☆ For a 50-space line, set your margins at 17 and 72.

  ☆ For a 60-space line, set your margins at 12 and 77.

  ☆ For a 70-space line, set your margins at 7 and 82.

If your machine has elite (102) type:

☆ For a 50-space line, set your margins at 26 and 81.

☆ For a 60-space line, set your margins at 21 and 86.

☆ For a 70-space line, set your margins at 16 and 91

As you probably remember, most people stop typing several spaces before the right margin. For that reason, a 50-space line is really about 55 spaces, a 60-space line is about 65 spaces, and a 70-space line is about 75 spaces. This is the reason for setting your margins 5 spaces wider than the line length you want. Now, set your margins for a 50-space line and insert a sheet of paper into your machine. You are ready to type your first letter.

BLOCK STYLE LETTERS TO TYPE

First Letter in the Block Style

Application

The first letter has 57 words in the body. Refer to Table 9-1 to see where to set margins. Set your margins. Start at the proper point down on the page.

In this letter the writer is the typist, so do not type reference initials.

Use the same format being used in the material from which you are copying. Your lines of typed material will *not* necessarily start and end at the same places they start and end in the book when you type the letters in this chapter.

Now, you are ready to type.

```
October 2, 1981

Box 100
The Tribune
1515 L St. N.W.
Largo, Maryland 20870

Dear Sir:

I am interested in, and I believe well qualified for,
the position you have advertised in The Tribune for a
"social psychologist." As you can see from my enclosed
resume, I have had considerable education and experience
in the field. If you need more information, I will be
happy to provide it.

Thank you for your consideration.

Sincerely,


R. F. Johnston


Enc.
```

Evaluation

Proofread your letter carefully. Correct all mistakes neatly. You should have typed the date line 22 lines from the top of the page. Did you type it at the right place? You should have used a 50–space line. Your margins should have been set at 17 and 72, if you have a pica (85) machine, or at 26 and 81 if you have elite (102) type on your machine. Did you set your margins at the right places?

Does your paper look like the material you copied from? You may have broken lines at different places but the basic format details should be the same. For example, you should have left blank lines after the date line, the inside address, and the salutation. In addition, you should have left blank lines between paragraphs, before the complimentary close, and before the enclosure notation. You also should have left three blank lines for the handwritten signature.

Did you do everything correctly? If so, you are ready to apply what you have learned. If you made any mistakes review the material on parts of the letter and letter placement at the beginning of the chapter. Then type the letter again before you move to the next Application.

Application

Answer the following questions about the letter you typed in the last Application.

1. What does the first line of the *inside address* say?

2. What is the *salutation?*

3. What is the *complimentary close?*

4. What does the *date line* say?

Evaluation

1. Box 100

2. Dear Sir:

3. Sincerely,

4. October 2, 1981

If you answered all of those questions correctly, you can recognize the important parts of a letter. If you missed any of the questions, review Figure 9-1.

Second Letter in the Block Style

Application

Now, you are ready to type the second letter in the block style. The body of this letter has 128 words. Use Table 9-1 to determine how far down on the page you should start typing and where to set your margins. Type the material in the same format as shown here. Remember that your lines will not necessarily start and end exactly where they start and end in this book.

Now, you are ready to type. Leave your paper in your typewriter when you finish typing the letter.

```
March 12, 1981

Captain L. Chicken Jones
Up and Down Airlines
9876 54th Str.
Baltimore, MD 21201

Dear Captain Jones:

On March 2, 1981, I spoke with Mr. Tommie Thompson, Manager
of your Lost and Found Office at Lost Nation Airport about
my missing luggage.  Mr. Thompson gave me a form to fill out
and promised that he would trace the luggage.  I had still
not heard anything by March 6, so I called Mr. Thompson.  He
told me that he was still tracing the luggage.  When I still
had not heard anything by March 10, I called Mr. Thompson
again.  He told me that he had sent my form to another office.

I know that you have procedures and I appreciate the fact
that you have problems.  However, I have one question for
you.  While you are shuffling papers what am I supposed to
use for underwear?

Sincerely,



R. F. Langstrom


RFL/me
```

Evaluation

You have probably guessed, by this point, why you left your paper in your typewriter. Well, you're right! Now you have a chance to proofread and to correct errors.

Did you use the correct format? You should have typed the *inside address* 19 lines from the top of the page. You should have set your margins at 12 and 77, if your typewriter has pica (85) type, or at 21 and 86 if it has elite (102) type. Measure the distance from your left margin to the end of the longest line you typed on the right. Does it measure 5 or 5½ inches? It should. If you used the correct format, that's great! If you are not doing the optional material that follows, you may go on to the Self-Test at the end of the chapter.

If you made mistakes, study the material at the beginning of the chapter carefully and then retype the letter.

You will have a chance to type more letters in Appendix C. The remainder of this chapter is *optional*. It covers typing letters in *modified block styles* and addressing envelopes, cards, and labels. If you are not doing the optional material, you may skip ahead to the next chapter on typing tables.

TYPING LETTERS IN MODIFIED BLOCK STYLES (OPTIONAL)

The modified block styles used in business frequently vary in one or more of three ways from the standard block style. All three of these variations appear in the letter shown in Figure 9-2.

```
                                        (1) October 8, 1980

        Mr. P. Cottentail
        2445 Elm Street
        Phoenix, AZ 85077

        Dear Pete:

        (2)    Thank you for your letter of October 2.  You
        told me all about the Block Style but I understand
        that many letters contain variations of that style.

            For example, this letter contains three
        variations.  First, the date line is typed so that
        it ends near the right margin.  The second variation
        is that in many business letters, new paragraphs are
        indented five spaces.  Finally, the complimentary
        close sometimes begins at the center of the page.

            I hope to see you again soon.

                        (3) Sincerely,


                        Susie Zylch

        SZ/me
```

Figure 9-2   Letter in Modified Block Style

Let's look at the variations one at a time.

1. The *date line* is often typed so that it ends near the right margin. The easiest way to find the right place for the date line is to move your carriage or element to the right margin. From that point, you should:

    (a) first, *backspace* five spaces to bring your paper to the point where the average line will end;

    (b) then say the date to yourself and *backspace* one time for each stroke;

    (c) and begin to type the date beginning at the point where you stopped backspacing.

2. The second variation is to *indent* for new paragraphs. Paragraphs in most business letters are indented five spaces, but sometimes they are indented more than that.

3. The third variation is to start typing the *complimentary close* and the *signature* near the middle of your paper. The middle of your paper is at space 42, if you have a pica (85) machine, or at space 51 if your typewriter has elite (102) type.

   Now you are ready to type more letters.

First Letter in a Modified Block Form

Application

Use all three variations. Type the letter from the following material. The *body* has 187 words. Leave your paper in the machine after you finish typing the letter.

```
                                             February 28, 1981

Occupant
3219 Larry Place
Boston, MA 06108

Dear Friend:

     Have you visited Washington recently?  It is a beautiful
city.  You can visit the Capitol, the White House, and the
Lincoln and Jefferson Memorials.  You can climb the steps of
the Washington Monument and visit the Kennedy Center, which is
a living memorial.  There are interesting tours of the Bureau
of Printing and Engraving, which prints money, and of the FBI.

     Visitors and scholars alike can visit Congress in session
and use the resources of the Library of Congress, the National
Archives and the Smithsonian Institution.  The Smithsonian has
eleven museums, including five art galleries.  The Air and
Space Museum is part of the Smithsonian.  Visitors can see
rocks that were collected from the moon and several of the
actual space suits worn by our astronauts.  The National Zoo
is also a part of the Smithsonian.

     Washington is easily accessible by several interstate
highways, is served by three major airports and by Amtrak,
Greyhound and Trailways.  It also has a subway system,
officially called Metro, but some people call it a lot of
other things too.

     I hope that you have an opportunity to visit Washington
soon.

                         Sincerely,


                         H. T. Crawford
```

Evaluation

Check carefully for mistakes and correct them neatly.

Does your letter resemble the material you copied from? The *date line* should have been 17 lines from the top of the page. Your margins should have been at 12 and 77, if your machine has pica (8b) type, or at 21 and 86 if it has elite (102) type. Measure your longest line and determine if it took up 5 to 5½ inches.

Did you indent new paragraphs five spaces? Did your date line end near the right margin? Did your complimentary close and signature start in the middle of the page? Remember a standard sheet of paper is 8½ inches wide. Use your ruler to check how close to 4¼ inches (half way across) your complimentary close started.

If you did everything right, that's tremendous. Move to the second letter below.

If you made mistakes, type again before you go on.

Second Letter in a Modified Block Style

Application

Use all three variations given in the previous letter. Type from the following material. The *body* of the letter contains 86 words.

October 25, 1981

```
Ms. Sussana McBee
1986 Broad Street
Pittsburgh, PA 15232

Dear Sue:

     It was great seeing you last month.  How long
had it been?  At least a year.

     I want to let you know that the conference we
talked about will take place right here in Annapolis
during the last week of January.  Will it be possible
for you to attend?  I hope so.  It will be a good
professional experience.  Besides, you won't have
to pay for a hotel.  You can stay right here with
me in the guest room.

     I hope you can come in January.

               Sincerely,


               Fred
```

Evaluation

Check your paper for mistakes and make neat corrections. You should have typed your *date line* 21 lines from the top of the page. Your margins should have been set for a 50-space line. If you have pica (85) type, you should have set your margins at 17 and 72. If your machine has elite (102) type, your margins should have been set at 26 and 81.

If you did everything right, that's tremendous. The next section on typing envelopes, cards, and labels is also optional. If you plan to skip that section, take the Self-Test at the end of the chapter before you move ahead.

If you made mistakes, review Table 9-1 and other appropriate material carefully and retype the letter.

TYPING ENVELOPES, CARDS, AND LABELS (OPTIONAL)

Use Table 9-2 to learn the names and dimensions of standard-size envelopes, cards, and labels and the points up and down and across where you should start typing.

Table 9-2   Placement Guide for Envelopes, Cards, and Labels

Name of Item	Dimensions	Start Address Lines from Top	Left Margin Pica (85)	Elite (102)
No. 10 envelope	9 1/2″ × 4 1/8″	13	42	48
No. 6 3/4 envelope	6 1/2″ × 3 5/8″	13	24	30
Many index file cards and some labels	3″ × 5″	10	20	24

Always single space the return address and start typing it in the upper left hand corner of the envelope, card, or label. You may either single space or double space the address. It is suggested that you single space addresses that are four lines long or longer.

Figures 9-3, 9-4, and 9-5 show the proportionate positions of addresses on envelopes, cards, and labels with pica (85) type. Our page size prevents us from showing these items full size. If you have elite (102) type, the side margins will be somewhat bigger.

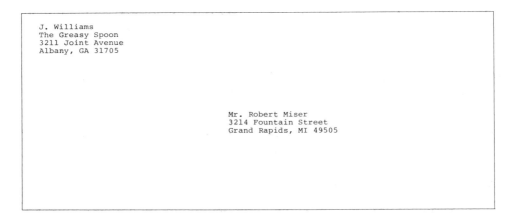

Figure 9-3 Address Typed on a No. 10 Envelope (9 1/2″ × 4 1/8″)

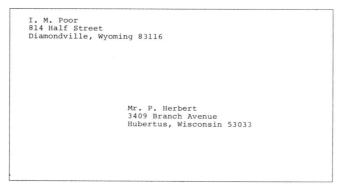

Figure 9-4 Address Typed on No. 6 3/4 Envelope (6 1/2″ × 3 5/8″)

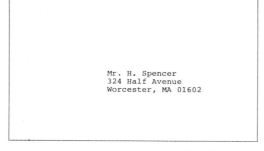

Figure 9-5 Address Typed on 3″ × 5″ Card or Label (no return address)

Application

Now, take four Number 10 envelopes, or cut paper into four pieces 9½ inches across by 4 1/8 inches up and down. On one envelope or sheet of paper first type your own name and address single spaced in the upper left-hand corner. This is your return address. Then type the following address.

```
Editor, Self-Teaching Guides
John Wiley & Sons, Inc.
605 Third Avenue
New York, NY 10016
```

Evaluation

Did it come out looking right (something like Figure 9-3)? Tremendous. Did you type your return address? In the right place? In the top left corner? Did you single space it? That's great!

　　　If you didn't do everything right, read the material on page 119 again and then type the address again.

Application

Now, try these addresses on your remaining three No. 10 envelopes or on paper cut to 9½ x 4 1/8 inches. In each case, use your own return address.

```
Occupant
1600 Pennsylvania Ave. N.W.
Washington, D.C. 20500

Mr. N. Bonaparte
Katz's Kosher Deli
Hopi Reservation
Hopi, AZ 85207

Sprinkle and Flood, Plumbers
1316 Old Drain Avenue
Newark, NJ 07101
```

Evaluation

Did those addresses look like the ones in Figure 9-3. If so, great! If not, try again.

Application

Take four 6 3/4 envelopes or sheets of paper cut into the same size and shape —6½ inches across by 3 5/8 inches up and down. On one envelope or sheet of paper type your own name and address as the return address, single spaced, in the upper left-hand corner. Then type the following address.

```
Ms. Kitty Kaiser
Dean of Student Affairs
Nick's University
Miami, Florida 33124
```

Evaluation

Does your envelope resemble the one in Figure 9-4? If so, great. You are ready to type three more envelopes.

If your envelope didn't look right, review Table 9-2 and try again. Then move to the next Application.

Application

Now, try these three addresses on your remaining envelopes or sheets of paper. Use your own return address in each case.

```
Mr. I. M. Obese
Fat Man's Liquor
11752 Georgia Avenue
Silver Spring, MD 20902
```

```
Mr. Joseph O'Donnell
O'Donnell's Car Care
8123 33rd St.
Baltimore, MD 21202
```

```
Mr. Horace Anderson
7842 Peachtree St.
Atlanta, GA 30301
```

Evaluation

Did your addresses look like the one in Figure 9-4? If so, you are ready for the next Application. If not, study Table 9-2 carefully and try again.

Application

Now, take four 3″ by 5″ index file cards or sheets of paper cut to that size. On one type the following address. Do *not* type a return address.

```
Ms. Harriet Rogers
First National Bank
7862 22nd St.
Buffalo, NY 14202
```

Evaluation

Does your card look like Figure 9-5? If so, you are ready to type the addresses below on the remaining cards. If your card didn't come out right, study Table 9-2 and try again.

Application

Now, type these addresses on 3" × 5" cards.

```
Ms. Sandy Wilson
3214 N. Vermont St.
Dallas, Texas 75207

Mr. Hubert Green
8413 South Green St.
Montpelier, Vermont 05602

Mr. W. T. Harder
Avis Rent-a-Car
245 Wilson Avenue
Philadelphia, PA 19104
```

Evaluation

Did your cards come out right? If so, that's very good. You are ready to take the Self-Test.

If they didn't come out right, study Table 9-2 and Figure 9-5 and try again. If you want to type more letters, turn to Appendix C.

SELF-TEST

This Self-Test will help you determine how well you have met the objective of this chapter and whether you are ready to go to the next chapter. An Evaluation guide follows.

Type the following letter in block style. Count the words and set up the letter properly. If you need help in setting up the letter, refer to Table 9-1 on page 112. Address the letter to your school or office. If you have no school or office, address it to your favorite restaurant. Use your home address as the return address. Use today's date. Sign and type your own name after the complimentary close.

Now, you are ready to type the body of the letter.

```
Dear Friend:

I just learned that there are several acceptable
styles in typing letters.  This letter is typed in
the block style.  There is no indenting at all in
the entire letter.  There are several other styles.
If you want to learn more about them, I suggest
that you purchase a copy of QUICK TYPING, A Self-
Teaching Guide.  It is published by John Wiley &
Sons, Inc. and is written by Jeremy Grossman.  It
is a very good book.

I hope to meet with you again soon.  Anyway, I'll
keep in touch.

Sincerely,
```

Evaluation Guide

The letter contains 91 words. According to the Letter Placement Guide (Table 9-1), you should have typed the date 21 lines from the top of the page. You should have set your margins for a 50-space line. If you have pica (85) type, the margins should have been set at 17 and 72. If you used a machine with elite (102) type, the margins should have been set at 26 and 81.

Everything in the letter should have started at the left margin. This includes the date, the inside address, the saluation, all paragraphs in the letter, the complimentry close, and the handwritten and typed signatures. Your letter should have a "balanced" appearance.

If you did everything right, that's great. You are ready to move to the last chapter of the book. If you made mistakes, review the portion of the chapter on the block style and type the letter again.

CHAPTER TEN

Typing Tables

In this chapter, you will learn to set up two-column tables, and you will have an opportunity to type several tables.

You will need a typewriter and about 20 sheets of standard-size typing paper.

OBJECTIVE

After completing this chapter, you will be able to:

- set up and type a two-column table.

TWO-COLUMN TABLE

Study Figure 10-1 first. Then come back and read the discussion to see how the spacing is computed.

Discussion of Figure 10-1

You should take the following steps to type the table in Figure 10-1.

Vertical Placement (up and down)

(1) Center the table up and down on the page, as follows.

   (a) Determine the number of lines your table will occupy. Include the blank lines when double or triple spacing.

   (b) Subtract the lines to be used from the total lines available on the page. The standard-size page has 66 lines up and down.
   In Figure 10-1 the table occupies 28 lines up and down on the page, including blank lines between typed lines. (Discussion continued on page 127.)

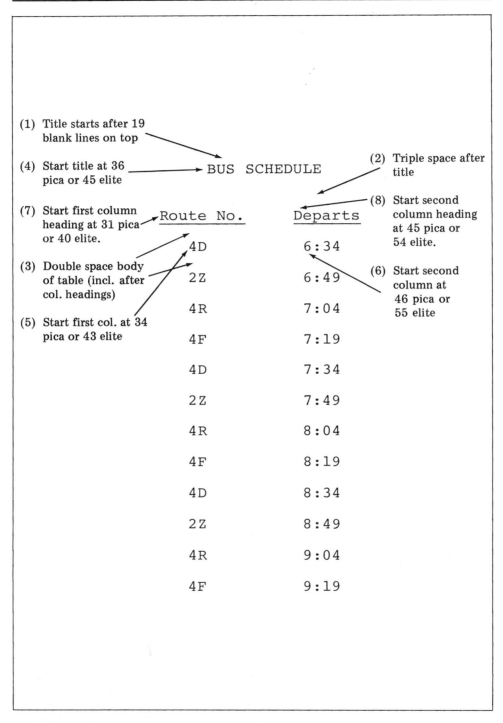

Figure 10-1 Two-Column Table. The numbers in parentheses are explained in detail in the discussion beginning on page 125.

66 lines available on page

– 28 lines to be used

38 unused lines

(c)   Take half the result in (b)

38 ÷ 2 = 19

Use this figure as the margin on the top of your page. If you were typing this table on a standard-size sheet of paper, you would leave 19 blank lines before you typed the title. (That is, you would start typing on the 20th line.)

(2)   Triple space between the title of the table and the column headings. (Triple space means that you type on every third line. There are *two* blank lines between each typed line.)

(3)   Double space between the column headings and the first line of the body of the table. Continue to double space throughout the remainder of the table. (Double space means that you type on every second line. There is *one* blank line between each typed line.)

Horizontal Placement (across)

(4)   Center the title across the page as follows:

(a)   Count the number of spaces in your title. Include blank spaces and punctuation.

BUS SCHEDULE

123456789012   12 spaces

(b)   Take half of that number.

12 ÷ 2 = 6.

(c)   Subtract the number you got in (b), 6, from the midpoint of your page.

If you have pica type, the midpoint of your page is at space 42.

42 – 6 = 36

Start typing the title at space 36.

If you have elite type, the midpoint of your page is at space 51.

51 – 6 = 45

Start typing the title at space 45.

(5)   Determine the starting point for the first column as follows:

(a)   Determine the number of spaces to be used in the longest item in the first column. *Ignore* column headings for now. Here, each of the entries takes up 2 spaces, so use the number 2 for the longest item.

(b)   Determine the space taken up by the longest item in the second column. In our example, all of the entries take up 4 spaces, so use the number 4.

(c)   Add the results of (a) and (b)

2 + 4 = 6

(d)   Add 10 to this total to allow for space between columns.

6 + 10 = 16

(e)   Take half of that number.

16 ÷ 2 = 8

(f)   Subtract the number in (e) from the midpoint of your page. If you have pica type, take 42 − 8, and set the left margin at space 34. If your machine has elite type take 51 − 8, and set your left margin at space 43.

Start typing the first column at the point you just set your left margin.

(6)   Determine the second column starting point as follows:

(a)   Determine the space where the longest item *ends* in the first column, and where the first available blank is. In our example, if you have pica type, each item in the first column starts at space 34 and ends at space 35. You, therefore, start counting the 10 blank spaces at space 36. If you are using elite type, the first column ends at space 45, and you begin the count at space 46.

(b)   Add 10 to the result in (a) to allow for the space between columns. If you have pica type the figure in (a) is 36. Add 10 to get 46. Set a tabulator stop at that point to begin your second column. If you have elite type, the number in (a) is 45. Add 10 to get 55. Set a tabulator stop at that point to begin your second column.

(7) and (8)

Placement of the column headings. You will soon learn how to compute the starting points for column headings. To complete the next Application, however, start the column heading "Route No." at space 31, if you are using a machine with pica type, or at space 40 if your machine has elite type. Start the second column heading at space 45 if your typewriter has pica type or at space 54 if it has elite type.

Application

Study very carefully the steps to type tables outlined on the previous pages. Then type the table from the following material. Do your work on a clean 8½″ x 11″ sheet of paper. Try to do it without referring to the discussion.

```
BUS  SCHEDULE

Route  No.    Departs

4D            6:34

2Z            6:49

4R            7:04

4F            7:19

4D            7:34

2Z            7:49

4R            8:04

4F            8:19

4D            8:34

2Z            8:49

4R            9:04

4F            9:19
```

Evaluation

How did your table come out? Does your table appear well centered? If so, great. If not, review Figure 10-1 and the discussion of it, and then retype the table.

TWO-COLUMN TABLES WITHOUT COLUMN HEADINGS

If you want to do so, review the material in the first part of this chapter before you start work on the following table.

Application

Do your best to type the table from just the material here without referring to the discussion. This table does not have column headings. Double space the table but triple space between the title and the first line. Leave 10 blank spaces between the columns.

After you type the table, compare your work with Figure 10-2.

Now, set up and type your table from the following information. Do your work on a clean 8½″ x 11″ sheet of paper.

```
TEST  SCORES
2287        92
3147        72
2486        84
1390        59
2476        93
3318        65
4217        94
5419        62
```

Check your work against Figure 10-2 and the discussion of it.

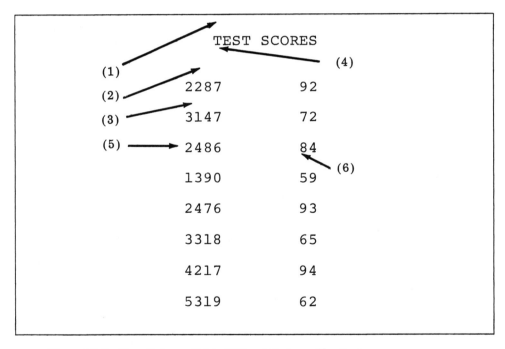

Figure 10-2   Two-Column Table Without Column Headings

Discussion of Figure 10-2

Since your work on 8½" x 11" paper will not look the same as it does in this book, you may want to check it against the discussion outline.

Vertical Placement

(1) You should have centered up and down. You should have had a top margin of 24 lines. (66 lines available minus 18 used leaves 48 unused). Half of this, 24, is the top margin. Refer to page 125 if necessary.)

(2) You should have triple spaced between the title and the first items in the columns.

(3) The remainder of the table should have been double spaced.

Horizontal Placement

(4) Did you center the title properly? It takes up 11 spaces. Did you take half of that figure (5½) and round off to 5? Then you should have backspaced 5 spaces from the midpoint of your machine and started typing the title at that point.

(5) Did you follow the correct procedure for computing the starting point of the first column? You should have done the following:

    (a) Determined that the longest item in the first column took up 4 spaces;

    (b) Determined that the longest item in the second column took up 2 spaces;

    (c) Added the numbers in (a) and (b) together (4 + 2 = 6);

    (d) Added 10 spaces between columns to the figure in (c) or (6 + 10 = 16);

    (e) Taken half of the number in (d) or (16 ÷ 2 = 8);

    (f) Subtracted the figure in (e) from the midpoint of your paper (resulting in space 34 if your machine has pica type or space 43 if it has elite type); and, finally you should have set your left margin at that point to begin your first column.

(6) How did you do in computing the starting point of the second column? You should have:

    (a) Determined where the longest item in the first column ends (37 for pica or 46 for elite) and the next available blank (38 for pica or 47 for elite);

    (b) Added 10 spaces to that figure (resulting in 48 pica or 57 elite); then, you should have set a tab stop at that point to begin typing the second column.

TWO-COLUMN TABLES WITH COLUMN HEADINGS

Now you will add column headings to the table you just typed in Figure 10-2. Look at Figure 10-3 as you follow the discussion of it.

TEST SCORES

(1)	#	Score	(2)
	2287	92	
	3147	72	
	2486	84	
	1390	59	
	2476	93	
	3318	65	
	4217	94	
	5319	62	

Figure 10-3   Two-Column Table with Column Headings

Discussion of Column Headings in Figure 10-3

(1)   Determine where to start the heading for the first column as follows:

   (a)   Take the longest item in the first column. Here all items are 4 spaces so we use the number 4.

   (b)   Count the number of strokes in the column heading. Here, there is only 1 stroke (#).

   (c)   Take the number from (a), and *subtract* the number in (b). Here, 4 – 1 = 3.

   (a)   Take half of the number in (c) and drop any fraction. Half of 3 is 1½. Round off to 1.

   (e)   Because the result is positive you type the column heading one space after your beginning point in the column. Take the number in (d) and start typing your column heading *1* space *after* your beginning point for the material in the column, 35 for pica, 44 for elite.

(2)   To determine where to start the heading for the second column you will follow a similar procedure, even though the heading takes more space than any item in the column:

(a) Take the longest item in the column. Here all items are 2 spaces long, so use the number 2.

(b) Count the number of strokes in the column heading. Here, the word "Score" takes up 5 spaces.

(c) Take the number from (a) and *subtract* it from the number in (b). Here, you have 2 − 5 which equals *minus* 3.

(d) Take half of that number and round off. Half of *minus* 3 is *minus* 1½. Round off to *minus* 1.

(e) Because the result is negative, you type the column heading one space before your beginning point for the column. Take the number in (d) and start typing your column heading that number of spaces *before* your beginning point for the rest of the material in the column. In our example, you should start typing the column heading 1 space *before* your beginning point for typing the remainder of the material in the column, or at 47 for pica, 56 for elite.

> If your column heading is <u>SHORTER</u> than the longest item in the column, type the column heading <u>AFTER</u> your beginning point for the rest of the column. If it is <u>LONGER</u>, begin typing the heading <u>BEFORE</u> your beginning point for the rest of the column.

Application 1

Type the table shown in Figure 10-3 on a clean sheet of 8½" x 11" paper. Remember that you have added column headings so that your table is longer vertically (up and down) than it was in Figure 10-2. Set your table up and type it from the following material.

TEST SCORES

#	Score
2287	92
3147	72
2486	84
1390	59
2476	93
3318	65
4217	94
5319	62

Evaluation

You should have had a top margin of 23 lines. (66 lines available minus 20 used leaves 46 unused. Half of this, 23, is the top margin.)

You should have started the column headings at the points listed in the discussion on pages 132 and 133. The spacing of the remainder of the table should be consistent with that in the discussion on page 131.

Application 2

Set up and type a table from the following material. Do your work on a clean sheet of 8½" x 11" paper. Leave 10 blank spaces between columns. Compare your work to Figure 10-4 and the discussion of it.

```
NEW  ACCOUNTS

Name                  Acct.  No.

Austin,  Richard      8472

Bowser,  B.B.         8473

Franklin,  B.         8474

MacDonald,  Arthur    8475

Morrison,  James      8476

Parker,  P.  T.       8477

Ronson,  P.  T.       8478

Sanders,  Harry       8479

Smith,  Louis  T.     8480

Thomas,  William      8481

Wilson,  T.  W.       8482
```

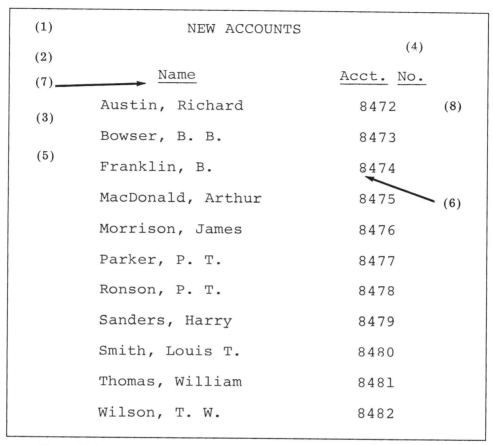

Figure 10-4   Second Two-Column Table with Column Headings

Evaluation

Again, since this book is not the same size as your paper, you should check your work against the following details.

Vertical Placement

(1), (2), and (3)

Remember that you should have triple spaced after the title and double spaced the remainder of the table. You should have computed that you start typing the title after 20 blank lines at the top of the page. (Your paper has 66 lines up and down. You needed to use 26 lines. That left you with 40 unused lines. Half of that number, 20 lines, should have been at the top of the page.)

Horizontal Placement

(4) The title occupies 12 spaces. You should have backspaced half of that number, 6, and started typing the title 6 spaces *before* the center of your paper—that is, at space 36 if you have pica type, or space 45 if you are using elite type.

(5) For your next step, you should have computed the starting point of the first column. The longest item is "MacDonald, Arthur," which takes up 17 spaces, including the comma and blank space between the last and the first names. Then you should have allowed 10 blank spaces between columns. All of the items in the second column occupy 4 spaces so you should have taken the number 4 for the number of spaces in the longest item in that column. Adding the figures together (17 for first column, 10 for blank spaces, 4 for the second column) you should have computed 31 spaces across on the page to be used. Then you should have taken half of that number (15½) and rounded it off to 15. You should have set your left margin and started typing the first column 15 spaces *before* the center of the page—that is, at space 27 if you have pica type, or at 36 if you have elite.

(6) Your next step should have been to compute the starting point for your second column. The first column ended at space 43 if you have pica type, or at space 52 if you are using elite type. You should have counted 10 spaces from the first available blank (44 for pica and 53 for elite) and started your second column at space 54 for pica type or 63 for elite type.

(7) Then you should have computed the starting point for the heading of your first column. In this example, the longest item in the column was 17 spaces. The column heading took up 4 spaces. Take 17 - 4 = 13. Take half of that number and round off. Half of 13 is 6½. Round off to 6. Start typing the column heading 6 spaces *after* your beginning point for the rest of the material in the column.

(8) Then you should have determined the starting point for the heading of your second column. Here the column heading took up 9 spaces. All items in the column used up 4 spaces. Take 4 and subtract 9 (4 minus 9 is *minus* 5). Take half of that number (*minus* 2½) and drop the fraction. This gives you *minus* 2. You should have started typing the heading 2 spaces *before* your beginning point for the rest of the material in the column.

SELF-TEST

This Self-Test will help you determine how well you have met the objective for this chapter and whether you have completed the course. (Additional work, which is optional, appears in the Appendices.) An Evaluation guide follows the Self-Test.

Look at the format of Figure 10-5 in the Evaluation. Leave 10 blank spaces between the columns. Compute the vertical and horizontal placement needed to center the table on an 8½″ x 11″ sheet of paper. Then type the table from the following material. Compare your work with Figure 10-5 and the discussion of it.

```
TEAM LEADERS

Name     Average

Ronson   .342

Smith    .338

Stone    .302

Johns    .296

Hubert   .295
```

Evaluation

Since your work was done on an 8½″ x 11″ sheet, you will need to check it against the details starting on the next page.

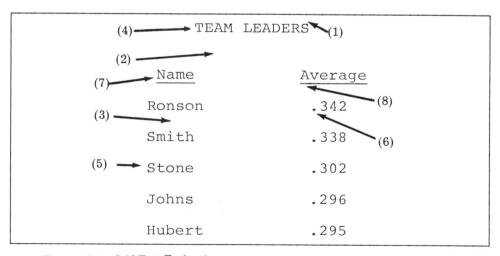

Figure 10-5   Self-Test Evaluation

Vertical Placement

(1), (2), and (3)

You have 66 lines up and down on the page. You use 14 of them in your table, including blank lines (66 – 14 = 52). Half of that figure, 26, should have been your top margin. Remember that you should have triple spaced after the title and double spaced the remainder of the table.

Horizontal Placement

(4)   To center the title across the page, you should have computed that it takes up 12 spaces. Then you should have taken half of this figure, 6, and backspaced that many spaces from the center of your page. You should have started typing the title from that point. If you have pica type, the center of your paper is at space 42. You should have subtracted 6 and started typing the title at space 36. If you have elite type, the center of your paper is at space 51. You should have subtracted 6 and started typing the title at space 45.

(5)   Next you should have computed the starting point for your first column.

    (a)   The longest items in the first column take up 6 spaces ("Ronson" and "Hubert").

    (b)   All items in the second column take up 4 spaces. (The decimal point counts, of course, as a space.)

    (c)   You should have added the figures in (a) and (b) to get 10. (6 in the first column plus 4 in the second column.)

    (d)   Then you should have added 10 to this figure for the spaces between columns (10 + 10 = 20).

    (e)   Then you should have taken half of this number (20 ÷ 2 = 10).

    (f)   You should have *backspaced* 10 spaces from the center of your paper, set the left margin, and planned to start typing the first column at that point. (If you have pica type, you should have taken 42 – 10 and planned to start typing at space 32. If you have elite type, you should have taken 51 – 10 and planned to start typing the first column at space 41.)

(6)   Then, you should have computed the starting point for your second column.

    (a)   The longest items in the first column should have ended at space 37 if you have pica type or at space 46 if you have elite type.

(b) Then, you should have added 10 spaces from the first available blank for the spaces between columns. (For pica type, 38 + 10 = 48. For elite type, 47 + 10 = 57.

You should have set your tabulator to stop at that point and planned to start typing the second column there.

(7) The next step should have been the computation of the column heading for the first column.

(a) First, you should have determined that the longest item in the first column occupies six spaces.

(b) Then, you should have determined that the number of strokes in the column heading is 4 (*Name* occupies four spaces.)

(c) Then, you should have taken the number in (a) and *subtracted* the number in (b) (6 – 4 = 2.)

(d) Then, you should have taken half of the number in (c). Half of 2 is 1.

(e) Next, you should have taken the number in (d) and started typing your column heading 1 space after the point where you planned to start typing the first column. If you have pica type, you should have planned to start the column heading at space 33. If you have elite type, you should have planned to start the column heading at space 42.

(8) Finally, you should have determined the starting point for the second column heading.

(a) You should have remembered (or determined) that all of the items take up 4 spaces. Therefore, you should have used the figure 4 for the longest item in the column.

(b) You should have determined that the column head "Average" occupies 7 spaces.

(c) Your next step should have been to *subtract* the amount in (b) from the one in (a) (4 minus 7 is *minus* 3).

(d) Then, you should have taken half of the amount in (c). Half of *minus* 3 is *minus* 1½. You should have rounded this off and ended up with *minus* 1.

(e) Finally, you should have taken the number in (d), *minus* 1, and spaced *minus 1* space (or *backspaced* 1 space) from the point you have planned to start typing the body of the second column. If you have pica type, you should have *backspaced* one space from the second column starting point (48) and started typing the column heading at space 47. If you have elite type, you should have taken 1 from the starting point (57) and started typing the column heading at space 56.

If your machine has pica type, your table should have been in the same proportion as the one in Figure 10-5. If it has elite type, your table should have had wider margins, but it should have been centered both horizontally and vertically.

How did you do? Was your table properly centered? If so, great! If not, study the material in the chapter carefully and then try again.

If you want more practice on timed writings, typing reports, typing letters, and/or want to learn to set up backing sheets for reports and letters, you may turn to the appendices which follow. Otherwise, you have completed your course. You made it!

Congratulations!!

APPENDIX A

More Timed Typings

In this Appendix you will have a chance to take more timed typings. Double space all of them and set your margins at 21 and 86 if you have elite (102) type, or at 12 and 77 if you have pica (85) type. Start and end each line where it starts and ends here. Do not type reference numbers. If you need help in computing your speed, turn back to pages 95 and 96 for one-minute computations and pages 97 and 98 for five-minute computations.

First One-Minute Timing

```
    I am almost finished with my typing course.  I do not yet      11

    realize how much I have learned.  I know the keyboard           22

    and all of the symbols in both the lower case and in the       33

    upper case.  I can also type business letters and do a         44

    pretty good job of setting up and typing tables.  When         55

    I complete this timing, I will see how fast I typed it.        66

    ----1----2----3----4----5----6----7----8----9---10---11---
```

Second One-Minute Timing

```
    Bus routes have been curtailed to end at the Metro stops.  As   12

    a result, people who are used to taking the bus from home to    24

    downtown now have to get off the bus and transfer to a Metro    36

    train.  At first, the combined bus and train passenger volume   48

    was less than the bus traffic alone was when the first trains   60

    on the six billion dollar Metro system started running.         71

    ----1----2----3----4----5----6----7----8----9---10---11---12
```

First Five-Minute Timing

```
    The Federal Government has spent tens of billions of dollars      2

on education in the past year.  One thing that is being             5

discovered is that just spending does not improve the quality       7

of education.  More care must be taken to be sure that             10

federal money is spent carefully on appropriate programs.          12

It has been discovered that many of the young people who           14

were enrolled in Head Start a few years ago lost most of           17

the Head Start they were supposed to get in the program.  It       19

has also been discovered that billions of dollars spent on         22

audio-visual equipment has been wasted because too many            24

teachers are not confident that they know how to operate the       26

equipment.  Therefore billions of dollars of equipment goes        29

unused.                                                            29

On the positive side, it has been determined that people who       31

are well motivated and want to learn can do so in spite of         34

tremendous hardships imposed on them.  And, they can learn         36

even if the government does not spend huge amounts of money        38

on education                                                       39
------------------1------------------------2----------------
```

Second Five-Minute Timing

```
    The typewriter as we know it has been in use for about one       2

hundred ten years.  At first, it was not designed for speed.        5

It was supposed to be an innovative form of printing.               7

Several different keyboards were tried.  The keyboard used         10

today is not an efficient one.  About fifty-six percent of         13

everything typed is typed with the left hand.  This is the         15

weaker hand for most people.  In addition, many of the most        18

used keys are on the top row instead of the home row.  The         20

only vowel key on the home row is the A.  It is on the weakest     23

finger of the left hand.  The most efficient possible              25

keyboard would look much different from the one in use             28

today.                                                             28
-------------------------1--------------------2---------------
```

Third Five-Minute Timing

```
If you are typing on a new typewriter, the chances are that it        2

is an electric machine.  Fewer manual typewriters are being           5

manufactured and sold than in the past.  When a person, a school      7

or an office buys typewriters they almost always buy electric        10

machines.                                                            10

It is much easier to type on an electric machine than on a           12

manual because the machine controls the touch.  On a manual          15

typewriter, if your stroking is inconsistent you are likely          17

to have light and dark strokes or skipping.  It is very              20

difficult to make such mistakes on electric machines.  It is         22

also much more difficult on an electric machine to have a flying     24

capital.  In short, you have to work much harder to make             27

many mistakes on electric typewriters than on manual typewriters.    29

If you learn to type on a manual typewriter, you should have         32

little.trouble getting used to an electric machine.  However,        34

if you learn to type on an electric machine and then have to         37

type on a manual, it would be a good idea to be ready for a          40

difficult adjustment.                                                41
-------------------------1-----------------------2-----------
```

Fourth Five-Minute Timing

```
In the past, if multiple copies of a letter were required, a        2
typist had to use carbon paper and make any corrections or          5
changes separately on each copy.  It was frequently difficult       7
to read the third or fourth copy.  Today, of course, carbon        10
paper is an endangered species.  It has largely been replaced      12
by copying machines.  A good copier can turn out an unlimited      14
number of copies all of which are readable.  If it is necessary    17
to make a change in the copy, the change can be made on the original  19
before it is copied by the machine.  There is no need to correct   22
each copy individually.                                            23
Modern equipment has also made it possible to store information    25
in automatic typewriters.  It is not necessary to retype an        28
entire manuscript for a final draft.  The unchanged portions       30
can be automatically typed and it is only necessary to retype      32
the material that is being changed.  If you want to                35
replace a four letter word with a ten letter one, you can simply   37
delete the old word and type the new one.  The machine can take    39
care of the spacing automatically                                  42
Today there are a number of correcting typewriters on the          44
market.  On these machines, it is possible to correct a mistake    47
as soon as it is made, almost without losing a beat.  If           50
you are taking a typing speed test, you can correct mistakes       52
in two or three seconds and you don't have to deduct from          54
your speed for mistakes.                                           55
------------------------1------------------------2--------------
```

If you want more practice in taking timings, you may repeat any of the timings in this appendix and/or those in Chapter 7. Otherwise, you have completed the timed writings.

Setting Up a Backing Sheet for Reports

This Appendix will help you set up a backing sheet to be used in report typing. You can place the backing sheet in back of the paper you type on to help you stay within the margins (top, bottom, right, and left).

Follow these steps to set up your backing sheet.

1. Set your *line-space regulator* at 1 for *single spacing*.

2. Make sure your *paper guide* is at zero.

3. Set your margins at 15 and 75 if you have pica (85) type, or at 18 and 90 if you have elite (102) type.

4. Insert a standard-size sheet of paper in your machine.

5. Bring your paper up to the point where you can just barely type on the paper, not on the cylinder. Then bring the paper up 9 lines and use the underline key to type a line between your left and right margins. (Nine lines is an inch and a half.)

6. Take the paper out of your machine. Put it back in on the same side with the line you just typed near the bottom of the page. Come up 6 lines from the bottom (start counting as in Step 5 above) of the page (1 inch) and type another line from the left margin to the right margin.

7. Bring up the paper 6 more lines (1 inch) and type another line from the left margin to the right margin.

   At this point, your paper should look proportionately like the illustration on the next page. Here you have the top and bottom margins and a line to warn you that you have only 6 lines left before you have to start a new page.

8. The next step is to connect the top and bottom lines, either with the typewriter by putting the paper in sideways and/or with a straight edge. After you connect these lines, all you have to do is use this sheet in back of your paper and stay within the margins. You will have a well-balanced appearing report.

   Your backing sheet should resemble Figure B-2 on page 147.

   You may want to use your new backing sheet to retype one or more of the reports on pages 105, 106, 107, and 108.

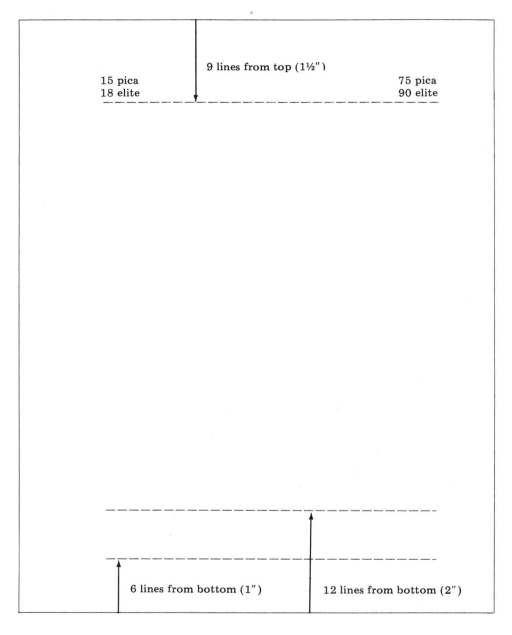

Figure B-1   Proportionate Sketch for Backing Sheet for Reports, Top and Bottom
Margins.

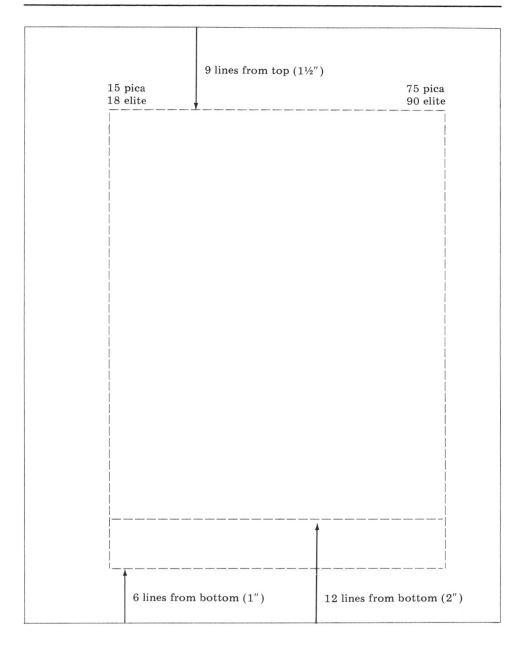

Figure B-2   Proportionate Sketch for Backing Sheet for Typing Reports, Right and Left Margins.

APPENDIX C

More About Letters

The material in the first part of this Appendix will show you how to set up a backing sheet which you may place behind your paper when you type letters. Then, starting on page 152, you will have an opportunity to type more letters. If you simply want more letters to type, you may use the Letter Placement Guide on page 112 and then skip to page 152. Otherwise, continue reading about the backing sheet below.

THE BACKING SHEET

The backing sheet will help you use margins that are "close enough" for most purposes. If you set up your backing sheet properly and stay within its margins, your letters will be acceptable for mailing. If you need *precise* form, you should use the Letter Placement Guide on page 112.

The backing sheet assumes that you will be typing on a letterhead. If you are not using a letterhead (and you will not be after the first page of a multi-page letter), leave a top margin of 9 lines. Otherwise stay within the margins of the backing sheet you are about to prepare.

To set up your backing sheet, follow these instructions:

1. Set your *line-space regulator* at 1 for single spacing.

2. Set your *paper guide* at zero.

3. Set your margins at 12 and 77 if you have pica (85) type, or at 21 and 86 if you are using elite (102) type.

4. Insert a standard-size sheet of paper in your machine.

5. Bring the paper up to the point where you can type the first line. Then bring the paper up 20 more lines. Next, use the underline key to type a line between the left and right margins. This will serve as the top margin for the *first page only* of your letter.

6. Take the paper out of the typewriter. Put it back in upside down. Make sure the typed side of the page still faces you. Come up 6 lines and type a line between the margins. This will serve as your bottom margin.

7. Bring the paper up 6 more lines and type a line between the margins again. This will serve as the warning line that you are coming close to the bottom margin. When you reach this line and you see you will not be able to complete the letter on the page, you should start on a second page. Always type at least two lines of the body of a letter on a new page. Do not start a new page for "Sincerely yours," or for one line and then "Sincerely yours."

8. The next step is to connect the top and bottom at the left and right margins. You may either put the paper in sideways and type or use a pencil and a straight edge to draw the lines. If your machine has pica (85) type, your backing sheet should look proportionately like the one illustrated on page 150. If you have elite (102) type, your paper should look proportionately like the illustration on page 151.

Remember that when you are not using letterhead paper you should leave a top margin of 9 lines. Otherwise, stay within your backing sheet lines.

You may use your backing sheet to type one or more of the letters starting on page 152 or to retype any of the letters in Chapter 9.

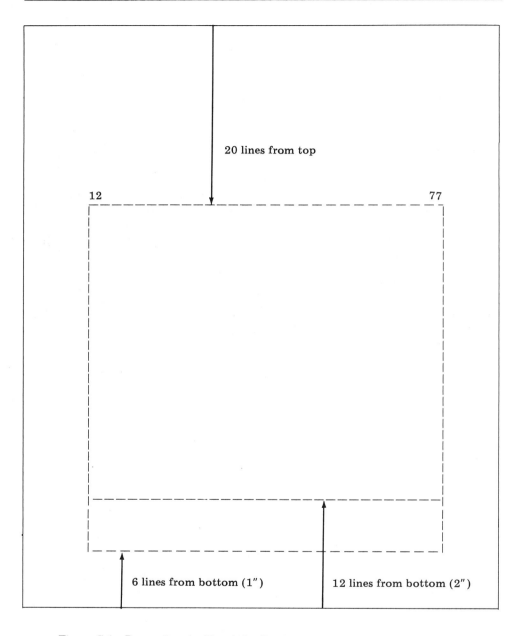

Figure C-1   Proportionate Sketch for Backing Sheet for First Page of Letters Typed on Pica Machine.

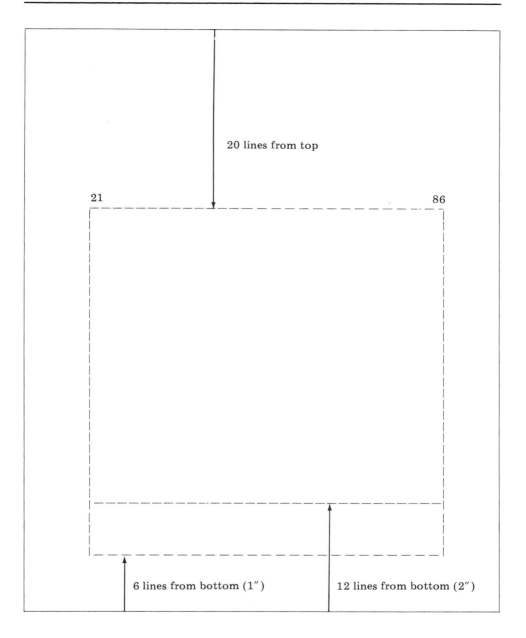

Figure C-2   Proportionate Sketch for Backing Sheet for First Page of Letters Typed on Elite Machine.

MORE LETTERS

Now, you will have an opportunity to type more letters. Use either the backing sheet or the table on page 112 as a guide. You may type in the block style or in one of the variations of it. Use your own name for the signature and your own address for the return address. Use today's date. Remember to *single space* the body of the letter.

Now you are ready to type:

Letter 1

Mr. Norman Harris
The CAB Corporation
8331 Slippery Fox Creek
Truman, Kansas 66777

Dear Mr. Harris:

As of the first of the year we are moving to our new location in the downtown area of the city. We hope that this will make it easier for you to come to our store.

During the first two weeks of January, we will sell everything at 20 percent off. We hope to see you and your family in our new store soon.

Sincerely,

Letter 2

Mr. Robert T. Cooper
Asst. to the Asst. Manager
Playtime, Inc.
4511 N. 34th St.
Omaha, Nebraska 68123

Dear Bob:

Mr. C. T. Rogers of the New York office will be in our area for the next three or four days. We are very happy to have him here. Please do what you can to make it possible for the people in your section to have a chance to meet with him.

Thank you.

Sincerely,

Letter 3

Mr. Jack B. Stalk
8473 Turnpike Rd.
Provo, Utah 84601

Dear Jack

I am sorry that I missed you last week. I thought that I would have several hours between planes. However, the first flight was late and I did not have the time to meet with you. I will make every effort to visit with you the next time I am in your area.

Yours truly,

Letter 4

Ms. Nancy Crickett
85 South Half Street
Pierre, South Dakota 57501

Dear Ms. Crickett:

You have had a past due balance for the past ninety days. If we do not hear from you within the next ten days, we will have to send your account for collection. This action will affect your credit rating.

We hope to hear from you very soon.

Respectfully,

Letter 5

Mr. Louis Johnston
2581 Elm Street
Anniston, Alabama 36201

Dear Mr. Johnston:

I wrote to you three months ago about my account, number 85247. I have not heard from you and my account has still not been corrected. I hope to hear from you this week so that it will not be necessary to make a formal complaint to the Consumer Protection Office.

Sincerely,

Index

NOTES